DOR

Keys to Unlock Answers from Heaven

SKP
SHEKINAH PRODUCTIONS

Cover Art and Book Design by Carol Smith
All Occasions: alloccasions2003@bellsouth.net

Back Cover photograph © 2007 Glamour Shots
Edited by Tasha Woodus & Cynthia Lawrence

Library of Congress Control Number: 2007909897

ISBN – 978-0-9802250-0-6

Shekinah Productions
P.O Box 278
Olive Branch, MS 38654

Printed in the United States of America

Dedication

This prayer manual is dedicated to my precious Lord and Savior Jesus Christ who imparted the desire, wisdom, motivation and endurance to complete this manual.

"…for He is faithful that promised" Hebrew 10:23

To my loving husband, Joseph, who has been a source of strength and has supported me with unconditional love, understanding and prayer during the many hours of preparation. Thanks honey, without you this manual could not have been birthed.

To my son and daughter, Christopher (Chris) and Konstance (Konnie), for their love, support and encouragement.

Acknowledgements

To my spiritual father and mother
Drs. Leo and Alma Holt, Pastors of Grace Christian Fellowship Church
International, Memphis, TN, for strong leadership and the impartation of
prayer.

To Carol Smith who has served as God's midwife for this manual
(Exodus 1:16-21).

To Darlene Hill and Tanya Glover who offered much support and
encouragement. Your labor of love will never be forgotten.

Table Of Contents

Introduction

Imagine for a moment, that you are a member of a prayer team at your church. You are all gathered to pray the evening prayer assignment given by your Pastor. Several of the team members have been asked to lead in prayer on different topics. You are one of the ones that have been asked to lead. Suddenly, the excitement about coming to prayer begins to diminish quickly as you are overcome with fear. Your heart began to beat faster and you become overwhelmed with thoughts such as, "I don't know what to say," "I can't pray like them," "God won't hear my prayers." Two others have already prayed before you, but you are so consumed with fear that you never heard their prayers. Then finally, it's your turn, and you open your mouth and nothing seems to come out right, you feel so inadequate, and once again the devil reminds you that you are not qualified to pray.

Many Christians struggle with questions about praying effectively and feelings of inadequacy in prayer. Does it seem that some Christians naturally have confidence in prayer? Have you noticed others who seem to have secrets in prayer that cause God to answer all of their prayers? Are there really secrets or keys to gaining such boldness and confidence in prayer? Are there scriptural things that a Christian can do to ensure answers from heaven each time they pray? It is God's desire that every Believer become a skillful, confident person of prayer. Prayer should be as easy as conversing with a close friend. "Keys to Unlock Answers from Heaven" will assist you in becoming stronger and bolder in prayer. You will learn the foundational keys to developing a scripturally based, sound prayer life and will be confident that all heaven hears and answers when you pray.

These and other questions have been asked throughout the history of Christianity: "Why does God answer some prayers while others seem to go unheard?" "What are the secrets to getting answers in prayer?" The subject of feeling inadequate in prayer is not new. In Luke chapter 11:1 the disciples had feelings of inadequacy in prayer and asked of Jesus: "Lord, teach us to pray." The disciples had noticed in their time with Jesus that He seemed always to get answers from the Father in prayer. However, the disciples had not been as successful so they went to the One that had mastered receiving answers to prayers. Just as the disciples did then, in this manual we will attempt to do the same by going to Jesus, the living Word of God, to receive keys to answers in prayer. In verses 2-4 of the same chapter of Luke, Jesus gave the disciples an outline or steps to prayer,

"When ye pray, say, Our Father which art in heaven, Hallowed be thy name. Thy kingdom come. Thy will be done, as in heaven, so in earth. Give us day by day our daily bread. And forgive us our sins; for we also forgive everyone that is indebted to us. And lead us not into temptation; but deliver us from evil."

Jesus intent was that we would use these scriptures as a method or example of how to approach the Father, rather than using the exact words each time in prayer. Next in verses 9-10 Jesus gives more instructions on prayer,

"And I say unto you, Ask, and it shall be given you; seek, and ye shall find; knock, and it shall be opened unto you. For everyone that asketh receiveth; and he that seeketh findeth; and to him that knocketh it shall be opened."

Lastly in verses 11-13 of Luke chapter 11 there is an example of how the Father responds to our request. According to these verses our Father in heaven responds to our prayer request similar to how our earthly father responds to us, but on a higher order, "If a son shall ask bread of any of you that is a father, will he give him a stone? Or if he ask a fish, will he for a fish give him a serpent? Or if he shall ask an egg will he offer him a scorpion?

If ye then, being evil, know how to give good gifts unto your children: how much more shall your heavenly Father give the Holy Spirit to them that ask him?" Here we see that the Father will only give us good gifts, things or requests that will not harm us. This prayer manual will look closely at some of the steps, guidelines and components to answered prayer. In addition there will be a review of some things that the bible indicates will either hinder or prevent answers to prayers.

A Life Without Prayer is Like a River Without Water...

CHAPTER
1

What is Prayer?

The art of prayer can be traced back to the book of beginnings, Genesis, when God talked with Adam and Eve in the cool of the day ("…And they heard the voice of the Lord God walking in the garden in the cool of the day…" Genesis 3:8). God has always desired a relationship with man as we note in Psalm 8:4 when the Psalmist David asks this question "What is man, that thou art mindful of him? And the son of man that thou visitest him?" David wanted to know what was so special about mankind that God not only thought of him but He also visited him. In fact we note in scripture that we were created to worship and commune with God. The communication between God and man was designed by God to be very simple. Since God made man in His image ("Let us make man in our image, after our likeness: and let them have dominion" Genesis 1:26) it was originally easy to communicate with God. But in Genesis chapter 3 man fell from his original state or fellowship with God and sin entered in and it became very difficult, uneasy for man to come into the presence of God. Therefore, instead of man running to God's presence, man became ashamed, guilty and condemned and ran from the presence of God. But the Father in His infinite wisdom sent His only begotten son, Jesus to redeem man back to God. Now through the plan of redemption man has the right to come boldly before the throne of grace and obtain mercy and find grace to help in a time of need (Hebrews 4:16). Prayer is communication, fellowship between God and man. It is God's desire that all Christians pray or communicate with Him. God did not design prayer as an art or a work, but rather as a way of life.

Just as there are different levels of communication between men, the same is true of levels of communication between God and man. The communication and relationship that a man has with his wife is totally different from the communication and relationship he has with his boss. There is definitely a greater intimacy between a husband and his wife. In like manner the level or depth of prayer is dependent on the level or depth of the relationship or fellowship with God. Always remember the greater the intimacy or depth of the relationship, the greater the liberty or freedom in prayer.

The language of prayer or communication with God is based on the Word of God. It is impossible to effectively communicate or have an intimate relationship with God if there is no knowledge of the Word of God. Jesus and God's Word are the same, they can not be separated. The Bible says in John 1:1 "In the beginning was the Word and the Word was with God, and the Word was God." With this scripture in mind we understand that the two are inseparable. The greatest foundation for a strong prayer life is the Word of God. The most effective person of prayer is the person that knows the Word of God, has intimate fellowship with the Father and His Son, and trusts the leading of His Holy Spirit.

PRAYER DEFINED

Prayer is communication that occurs between man (mankind) and God. The communication that God responds quickly to is the instructions that He left for us in the bible. God designed prayer as a means of communication between Himself and mankind. God also designed prayer as a means for man to create Heaven on earth by the speaking or praying forth of God's Word. Prayer is one of the most powerful means of changing events in the earth. Through prayer the kingdom of God is brought into the earth and the

Will of the Father is done on earth as it is in Heaven (Matthew 6:10, "Thy kingdom come. Thy will be done in earth as it is in heaven"). This powerful communication tool of prayer is one of the most under utilized resources that God has given unto the church. Man, through prayer, has the ability to totally change his world or to create a new one (Hebrews 11:3 – 'Through faith we understand that the worlds were framed by the Word of God").

INVITATION TO LIFE

To be an effective person of prayer the first step is to have a relationship with the Lord and Savior, Jesus Christ. The Bible tells us that "whosoever shall call upon the name of the Lord shall be saved" (Romans 10:13). Romans 10:9 say that "if we confess with our mouths and believe in our hearts the Lord Jesus Christ, we shall be saved." If you have never confessed Jesus as Lord and Savior of your life and would like to establish a relationship with Him, then I would like to offer you an invitation of a life time. Today you can take the initial step of establishing a relationship with the Lord Jesus Christ by praying this prayer out loud:

PRAYER

I confess that I am a sinner and that I need a Savior. I believe that Jesus is the son of God and that He died on the cross for my sins and that God the Father raised Him from the dead. I confess my ineffectiveness and ask now that Jesus would come into my heart and be my Lord and Savior. Jesus I now surrender my will totally to your Will and acknowledge that I am nothing without You. I denounce all the powers and strongholds of Satan in my life and yield myself totally to Jesus. Thank you Father that I am now of the household of faith and can partake of all the benefits of Your Kingdom. Thank you, Jesus for being my Lord and Savior. Amen

Now you are ready to begin your new relationship with the Lord Jesus Christ through a life of prayer.

SCRIPTURE REFERENCE:

Genesis 3:8

Psalm 8:4

Genesis 1:26

Hebrews 4:16

John 1:1

Hebrews 11:3

CHAPTER QUESTIONS

1. Where in scripture do you find the first biblical account of God talking with man?

   Genesis 3:8 God walking in the cool of the day communicating to Adam after he'd eaten from the tree of knowledge.

2. What incident caused prayer to become difficult?

   The fall of man

3. The foundation for prayer is?

   The Word Of God

4. What powerful communication tool is most under utilized by the church?

   Prayer

"*The Desire of the Righteous Shall Be Granted...*"

PROVERBS 10:24

CHAPTER 2

Key Components Of Answered Prayer

In my study of receiving answers in prayer I have determined that there are several key components to gaining answers. For the purpose of this study we will discuss seven necessary components:

    I.   The Father
    II.   The Son
    III. The Holy Spirit
    IV. Faith
    V.   Angels
    VI. The Blood of Jesus
    VII. Timing of God

THE FATHER

According to scripture the Father is the one who answers prayer. He is the one who gave us the pattern and the guidelines for how we should pray and how He would answer our prayers. According to Isaiah 55:10-11, the Father says:

"For as the rain cometh down and the snow from heaven, and returneth not thither, but watereth the earth, and make it bring

forth and bud, that it may give seed to the sower and bread to the eater: so shall my word be that goeth out of my mouth: it shall not return unto me , but it shall accomplish that which I please, and it shall prosper in the thing whereto I sent it."

God answers prayers that are inspired of Him. He answers prayers that line up with the Word of God. The scripture also notes in Psalm 37:4 "Delight thyself in the Lord and he shall give thee the desires of your heart." The Father in His infinite power first gives a desire and then He answers the desire that came from Him in the first place. Psalms 21:2 says "Thou has given him his heart's desire, and has not withholden the request of his lips." Also in Proverbs 10:24 we see that "...the desire of the righteous shall be granted." In Matthew 18:19 we note that although we pray the prayer of agreement in the earth, it is ultimately the Father in Heaven who answers, "Again I say unto you, that if two of you shall agree on earth as touching anything that they shall ask, it shall be done for them of my Father, which is in heaven." It is the words of the Father, spoken by the Believer in prayer, which the Father will respond to with an answer. In John 6:63 Jesus said "the words I speak unto you, they are spirit, and they are life." There is great power in speaking and praying the words of the Father. The Father's words, which are the words of the Bible, spoken in faith bring great deliverance and power into the circumstances of life. Although it is the Father that answers our prayers from Heaven, we must include the other key components to make sure that the answer is manifested in the earth. Remember Jesus said that whatever we ask the Father in His (Jesus) name He would do it for us. So although we ask the Father we must include Jesus in the request. In seeking answers to our prayer we must remember Luke 12:32 "Fear not little flock; for it is your Fathers good pleasure to give you the kingdom." The Father wants to answer our prayers that line up with the Word of God.

THE SON

There can be no answered prayer without the Son. Jesus according to scripture is "the image of the invisible God, the firstborn of every creature: for by Him were all things created that are in heaven, and that are in earth, visible and invisible, whether they be thrones, or dominions, or principalities, or powers: all things were created by him and for him (Colossians 1:15-16)." The Father designed it so that no prayer could be answered unless it was done in the name of Jesus, "And whatsoever ye shall ask in my name, that will I do, that the Father may be glorified in the Son, if ye shall ask anything in my name, I will do it." (John 14:13-14). Additionally, according to the Word of God in John 1:1-3, 14, Jesus is the Word in the flesh,

"In the beginning was the Word, and the Word was with God, and the Word was God. The same was in the beginning with God. All things were made by him; and without him was not anything made that was made... And the Word was made flesh, and dwelt among us, and we beheld his glory, the glory as of the only begotten of the Father, full of grace and truth."

Jesus is the Word and there can be no answered prayer without the Word of God, "And He was clothed with a vesture dipped in blood: and his name is called The Word of God." (Revelations 19:13) Jesus also gave his disciples and all believers instructions for prayer while he lived in the earth. In John 16:23-24, Jesus said that we should ask Him nothing, but that we should ask the Father in His name, "And in that day ye shall ask me nothing, Verily, verily, I say unto you, whatsoever ye shall ask the Father in my name, he will give it you. Hitherto have ye asked nothing in my name: ask and ye shall receive that your joy may be full." Jesus said if we ask the Father anything in His name the Father would give it to us that our joy would be full. When we receive an answer to our prayer our joy is full because we received what we asked of the Father. The Father and the Son are one. You can not have answered prayer without the two working together. According to Colossians 1:18 God gave Jesus preeminence to the Church, "And he is the head of the body, the church: who is the beginning, the firstborn from the dead; that in all things he might have the preeminence." Jesus is the head of the Church and the Church must take all instructions from the head. As we seek the Lord for answers in prayer we must always remember that although we pray to the Father it is only in Jesus' name that we will effectively receive the answers that we so desire.

THE HOLY SPIRIT

The Holy Spirit is the Spirit of the Father in the earth. The Holy Spirit is the performer of the Word of God. The Father is in Heaven, Jesus also is in Heaven seated at the right hand of the Father making intercession for the saints (Hebrews 7:25, 10:12), but the Holy Spirit is in the earth. As Jesus was about to leave the earth He introduced His disciples to the Holy Spirit. Jesus said in John 16:7, 13, "It is expedient for you that I go away: for if I go not away, the Comforter will not come unto you; but if I depart, I will send him unto you. Howbeit when He, the Spirit of Truth, is come, he will guide you into all the truth: for he shall not speak of himself; but whatsoever he shall hear, that shall he speak: he will show you things to come." Jesus was saying to us that the Holy Spirit or Spirit of Truth would be in the earth after Jesus left and that He, the Holy Spirit, would guide us into all truth. The Holy Spirit will only speak or perform what He hears the Father and Son say. The three are in perfect agreement. The Father answers the prayer according to His Word, Jesus is the Word and the Holy Spirit can only perform that which is of the Word. All three are equally important, however if you do not know or speak the Word in prayer, the Father will not hear your prayer and the Holy Spirit won't act on it. To obtain consistent answers in prayer there must be a strong Word base and the wisdom to use it appropriately. Yes, the Holy Spirit is the one to lead us into all truth but, how does He lead us? He leads according to the scriptures, the Word of God. The Holy Spirit not only leads us but He is also the One who teaches us the Word of God and brings the Word of God to our remembrance. Note in John 14:26, "But the Comforter, which is the Holy Ghost, whom the Father will send in my name, he shall teach you all things, and bring all things to your remembrance." What are the things that the Holy Spirit brings to our remembrance? The answer of course is the Word of God. However, if we do not study, read and meditate on the Word of God, how can He bring it to our remembrance? The word remembrance indicates that it is something that we have heard before (remember is defined according to Webster's as "to recall something to mind or become aware of something that had been forgotten.") In order for the Holy Spirit to bring things to our remembrance during prayer, trails, and our everyday life, we must first have heard or read the Word of God. Remember "Faith cometh by hearing and hearing by the Word of God" (Romans 10:17). After we have heard and read the Word then we must believe and trust the Holy Spirit to perform that Word. The Holy Spirit is definitely a key component to gaining answers in prayer. He is the One who reveals to us what the Will of the Lord is concerning our personal lives. Once He reveals God's plan, then we can pray God's perfect will for our situation into manifestation.

Knowing and following the voice of the Holy Spirit is very important in order to walk in the plan of God for your life. Several years ago I made a choice to leave my management job of 18 years as a Registered Nurse. The idea to leave my job was not Gods plan but my choice. Therefore, because He is a perfect gentleman and will not override your will, He allowed me to leave. After several years of struggling financially outside of the will of God I returned to work as a staff nurse at a psychiatric hospital. I was very happy in my new role because I had returned back to the path God had for my life at that time (work!). One morning during my prayer time the Lord spoke to me about returning to a role in management. I became very excited about the Holy Spirit's leading and began to agree with Him. I agreed with Him according to His word that His will would be done in my life on earth as it was in Heaven. After I prayed, I began filling out applications all over the city. Unfortunately, I became very frustrated when every door I approached for a position was shut in my face. I could not understand why the Lord would tell me to go back into management but would not open a door. I began to blame others for blocking my promotion due to jealousy. As usual when I don't understand or become frustrated I began to talk to God about it. I said "Father it is not fair that you would promise me something and then just because someone else doesn't like it they can block it." I went on to say that "if a human can stop Your divine plan for my life than something is really wrong with this set up." After I cried and fussed and poured my heart out to God He said something to me that I will never forget. God said "no person can stop your blessing or promotion, only you can do that." You see I discovered that as long as my heart is right toward God and others, no unforgiveness, no bitterness, no hurt, no flesh can prevent what God has for me. God said the reason I didn't get the other jobs was because they were not my jobs. After I heard from the Lord I begin to settle down and wait on God's next directive. Often times we move to quickly without proper instructions. We must wait on the Lord for each step and then obey Him. Many times the next step is to simply wait for the Lord to move. So, I waited for the Lord and you guessed it, He moved, and a position in management at the same hospital I worked at came open. I was initially reluctant to accept the position when it was offered to me because it was actually less money than I was making. But I had the peace of God that the new position was His will for my life. I accepted the position and in less than 6 months I received three pay raises. Glory to God!

FAITH

The next key component that we must have to gain answers to our prayers is faith. The scripture says, "Now faith is the substance of things hoped for, the evidence of things not seen" Hebrews 11:1. "Without faith it is impossible to please God; for he that cometh to God must believe that He is, and that he is a rewarder of them that diligently seek Him." Hebrews 11:6. Faith is the component that the believer must have. Believing God and standing in faith is the hardest task for the believer in receiving answered prayer. The scriptures says in Mark 9:23 "If thou canst believe, all things are possible to him that believeth." Think about it, anything that you are asking God for, if it lines up with the will of God, you can have it but you must believe in order to receive it. During Jesus' ministry in the earth He placed great emphasis on belief, having faith in God. The Father, the Son and the Holy Spirit will always do their part but, as Believers we must remain faithful and unwavering in doing our part. The Holy Trinity is looking to us, the Believers, who have legal rights here in the earth. The Believers are the ones who have been given all authority in heaven and in the earth through our Lord and Savior, Jesus Christ. Therefore we must take our place of authority and stand strong in faith, unwavering, looking for answers to our prayers. When we do not receive answers to our prayers, often it is due to our lack of faith. Jesus said in Matthew 17:20 to His disciples when they asked why they couldn't cast the devil out, "Because of your unbelief: for verily I say unto you, If ye have faith as a grain of mustard seed, ye shall say unto this mountain, remove hence to yonder place; and it shall remove and nothing shall be impossible to you." Again Jesus said in scripture "And all things, whatsoever ye shall ask in prayer, believing, ye shall receive" (Matthew 21:23). The Father answers prayer from Heaven, Jesus is the living Word, and the Holy Spirit is the performer of the Word. But the believer must have faith, or believe in the Word of God in order for the prayer to come to pass. The first step for the believer is to believe that what God said is true. Romans 4:3 say that "Abraham believed and it was accounted unto him as righteousness." When we stand in faith and believe God for answers to our prayer we must learn to be like the Father of Faith, Abraham, who "staggered not at the promise of God through unbelief; but was strong in faith, giving glory to God, and being fully persuaded that what he had promised, he was able to perform." (Romans 4:20, 21).

There have been many opportunities for me to stand in faith during very difficult times. During those difficult times the Word of God was the only thing I had to hold on to. For example, I can remember a day when suddenly things went from not good to horrible in less than an hour. On this day my husband and I had just left church and were driving home on the expressway. I remember laying back in my seat basking in the glory of the service we had just had at church. It seemed that day the service was especially anointed and I enjoyed every moment. Little did I know that I was about to be tested like never before. We had been on the expressway less than 10 minutes when the car we were driving began to go out. We had to quickly move to the side and have someone come to tow it. The other vehicle we had at home was already broken down and another vehicle had already been repossessed. When we finally got home our utilities had been turned off and we had no money to turn them back on. I called my job to say I had no transportation to get to work and that I would not be in. They informed me that if I did not show up that I was fired. My teenaged daughter looked at me as if to say why serve a God who has allowed all of these bad things to happen to us. This is an actual account of occurrences. You see there will come a time in your life when the Word of God will have to be real, alive, not just a confession. It seemed we had no way out and no one to help. We had to trust God, the Word had to be true or we would not make it. So, what did I do? When I walked in my door I sat in a chair in my living room and began to ponder what to do. The strangest thing came to my mind in the midst of my trail. I remembered that my first lady at church had a speaking engagement that evening. I also recalled that my Pastor had said many times before "if you take care of God's business He will take care of yours." I began to put what I heard my Pastor say into action, I prayed that God would heal, deliver and work miracles through His servant at that meeting. While I was praying I totally forgot the circumstances of my life and was totally focused on Gods plan for that night. After praying I began to praise God for turning the situation in my home around. I then found a flash light and sat down and began to read the Word. I made a decision that day like the three Hebrew boys that whether God delivers or not I would still serve Him. The lights were turned on later that day but for several months we had to ask someone to pick us up for church, work or school. This was a very difficult time but, we purposed as a family to remain committed to God. We never missed church, we never blamed our God but, we trusted Him. Within a couple of years we went from having no transportation to four vehicles. We learned in whatever state to be content but, we also learned that God's Word is true and if you only believe He will bring you out.

ANGELS

The most under utilized of the six key components of answered prayer is the effective use of angels. Throughout the Bible, Old and New Testament, there is much discussion about the ministry of angels. The believer is to solicit the help of angels in prayer. In Psalm 103:20-21 the scripture say's, "Bless the Lord, ye angels that excel in strength, that do his commandments hearkening unto the voice of his word." So according to scripture the Angels do God's commandments, they hearken (or listen) to the voice of His Word. My God, when the angels hear the words of the Almighty God, they hearken, they stand up, they listen, and they go to work. It is important that we speak or pray God's words in prayer, otherwise the angels have nothing to work with and the Lord can't perform our prayer. Hebrews 1:14 says, "Are they not all ministering spirits sent forth to minister for them who shall be heirs of salvation." Because we are heirs of salvation God has assigned angels to minister for us and to us according to His Word. In my study of the use of Angels in prayer, I have identified at least four areas in prayer that Angels are used to cause our prayers to be more effective. Listed below are the four areas that will be discussed further for the purpose of this study:

1. Angels are Messengers who bring information or give instructions regarding future events.
2. Angels provide protection and strength.
3. Angels assist in release from bondage or captivity.
4. Angels are active in Spiritual Warfare and execution of the judgment of God.

Angels are Messengers of Information or Instructions

There are several accounts in the Bible; Old Testament and New Testament where angels were used by God as Messengers to bring information or to give instructions to His servants. In Daniel 10:12-13 we see the Angel came to bring information to Daniel about the future. This scriptural account of Angelic assistance gives us an idea of how Angels work to assist the Believer in prayer, "Then said he unto me, Fear not Daniel: for from the first day that thou didst set thine heart to understand, and to chasten thyself before thy God, *thy words* (my emphasis) were heard, and I am come for *thy words* (my emphasis) (remember angels hearken at the word of God, Daniel was praying the word of God). "But the prince of the kingdom of Persia withstood me one and twenty days: but, lo, Michael, one of the chief princes came to help me." We note in scripture that Michael is the archangel of spiritual warfare ("Yet Michael the archangel when contending with the devil" Jude 1:9, "And there was war in heaven: Michael and his angels fought against the dragon." Revelation 12:7). Angels only respond to our words that are in line with the Word of God. The spoken Word of God is used as a weapon by the angels of God to gain victory in prayer. Again in Luke 1:11, 13 we see an angel showing up on the scene with information about the birth of John the Baptist to his father, Zacharias, "And there appeared unto him an angel of the Lord standing on the right hand of the altar of incense… But the angel said unto him, fear not, Zacharias: for thy prayer is heard; and thy wife Elisabeth shall bear thee a son, and thou shalt call his name John." The angel, Gabriel, also was sent to the virgin Mary to inform her of her coming pregnancy with the Messiah, "And in the sixth month the angel was sent from God unto a city of Galilee, named Nazareth, to a virgin espoused to a man whose name was Joseph … And the angel came in unto her, and said, Hail thou that are highly favored, the lord is with thee: blessed are thou among women." "And the angel said unto her, Fear not, Mary: for thou has found favor with God. And behold, thou shalt conceive in thy womb, and bring forth a son, and shalt call his name Jesus" (Luke 1:30, 31). In the New Testament again we note in Acts 10:3-6, an Angel brought information to Cornelius giving him directions on where to go to receive salvation. "..He saw in a vision evidently about the ninth hour of the day an angel of God coming in to him, and saying unto him, Cornelius, and when he looked on him, he was afraid, and said unto him, Thy prayers and thy alms are come up for a memorial unto God. And now send men to Joppa, and call for one Simon whose surname is Peter: He lodgeth with one Simon a tanner, whose house is by the sea side: he shall tell thee what thou oughtest to do." We note that although angels do not lead men to Christ they can direct men to the right person and place to receive salvation. The angel came with information and gave very specific instruction to Cornelius after he had prayed.

Angels Provide Protection and Strengthen

In Genesis 3:24 God used the Angels to block the entrance into the garden of Eden after Adam and Eve sinned, "So he drove out the man; and he placed at the east end of the garden of Eden Cherubims, and a flaming sword which turned every way, to keep the way of the tree of life." Here the angels were used to guard and protect. Also, in Psalm 91 the angels are used to protect the believer, "For he shall give his angels charge over thee, to keep thee in all thy ways. They shall bear thee up in their hands, lest thou dash thy foot against a stone." Angels are also used to minister and strengthen those who have endured great testing as we see with Jesus in Matthew 4:11 "Then the devil leaveth him, and, behold, angels came and ministered unto him." Jesus after going through much testing and warfare was ministered unto by the angels. Also we note in II King 6:16-17 where the servant of Elisha was concerned about the size of the army which was coming against he and his master, Elisha prayed that the Lord would open his servant's eyes to see the number of angels that were there to assist them in battle:

"...And he answered, Fear not: for they that be with us are more than they that be with them. And Elisha prayed , and said, Lord, I pray thee, open his eyes, that he may see, And the Lord opened the eyes of the young man; and he saw; and behold, the mountain was full of horses and chariots of fire round about Elisha. What a blessing to know that we have angels assigned from God to protect our lives.

We know scripturally God has given us each guardian angels. Although we may not always see them, we know by faith that they are present. Just as God opened the eyes of Elisha's servant to see the angels, He will at time open our eyes to see our angels to bring comfort. One particular instance comes to mind when I recall seeing my angel. About six years ago I had come under attack in my body with different symptoms such as, stomach pain, nausea, headaches, etc. The devil would frequently speak and say that he was going to kill me or that I would have to be hospitalized. Usually I would bind the assignment and trust God. This particular night I had been severely attacked and was having chest pains. As I prayed and rebuked the pain it would not leave but seemed to get worse and worse. The enemy was speaking to my mind again that he was going to kill me. I began to sense fear grip my heart but, I kept praying. As I lay down in my bed confessing the Word, I gently closed my eyes. Just as I began to close my eyes I saw standing to the side of me at the head of my bed a huge angel. He was standing tall and strong with his arms folded in strength and authority like a guard. He looked as if he was strong enough to stop anything or anybody. The peace of God fell on me and I fell asleep. From that day forward I never feared the voice of the devil speaking that he was going to kill me because I would always remember the height and strength of that angel. Praise God! God will sometimes reveal angels to us but we never pray to see angels, it's according to His will.

Angels are used in Releasing People from Bondage or Captivity

Amazingly we find in scripture that Angels actually assist in the literal physical and spiritual release of people. There are at least two occasions in Acts where the Apostles were physically released from prison by Angels.

> ***Acts 5:19 "...But the Angel of the Lord by night opened the prison doors, and brought him forth and said: Go stand and speak in the temple to the people all the words of this life... But when the officers came, and found them not in the prison, they returned, and told, saying, The prison truly found we shut with all safety, and the keepers standing without before the doors: but when we had opened, we found no man within."***

Praise the Lord! We see here that the angel of the Lord released the Apostle from prison with the guards still standing at the door and the lock still in place. The guards had never left the door. I am not sure how that could have happened but I know that it did happen because it is in the Bible. I also believe that if it happened then it can happen now because the word says in Hebrew 13:8 that "Jesus Christ the same yesterday, today and forever more." I know that if God did it once He can do it again, but the Believer must believe God's Word and ask in prayer according to what we see in the Word of God. This account about the Angel of the Lord releasing the Apostle from prison is not a story or an allegory; this is an actual documented account of the power of God activated through prayer. We see the Angels at work again in Acts 12:6-8, 11-16 as the saints were praying:

> *"...the same night Peter was sleeping between two soldiers, bound with two chains: and the keepers before the door kept the prison, and behold the Angel of the Lord came upon him, and a light shined in the prison and he smote Peter on the side and raised him up, saying, arise quickly and his chains fell off from his hands. And the Angel said unto him, Gird thyself, and bind on thy sandals, and so he did and he saith unto him; cast thy garment about thee, and follow me... And when Peter was come to himself, he said, now I know of a surety, that the Lord hath sent his angel, and hath delivered me out of the hands of Herod, and from all the expectation of the people of the Jews... And when he had considered the thing, he came to the house of Mary the mother of John, whose surname was Mark; where many were gathered together praying. And as Peter knocked at the door of the gate, a damsel came to hearken, named Rhoda. And when she knew Peter's voice, she opened not the gate for gladness, but ran in, and told how Peter stood before the gate. And they said unto her, thou art mad. But she constantly affirmed that it was even so. Then said they, it is his angel. But Peter continued knocking: and when they had opened the door, and saw him, they were astonished."*

As the saints were praying the Lord sent an Angel to release Peter from Prison. This time Peter was not alone in prison, (the guards knew he had gotten out before) He was sleeping with two guards, one on each side; he had two chains, instead of one this time, plus the guards were outside the door. But we thank God, through prayer; God can release us from any situation no matter how hopeless or impossible it appears.

Angels are used in Spiritual Warfare and Execution of the Judgment of God

There are several examples in scripture, Old and New Testament where the Lord uses His angels in spiritual warfare or to execute His judgment. We have already noted how in Daniel the Arch Angel Michael came to war against the Prince of Persia. Although there was already an angel there warring against the Prince of Persia to allow Daniel's prayer to come through, Michael came as reinforcement and then Daniel was able to receive the answer in prayer he sought. Jesus said in the Garden that he could ask his Father to send legions of Angels when the multitude with Judas came to take him, "Thinkest thou that I cannot now pray to my Father, and he shall presently give me more than twelve legions of Angels?" (Matthew 26:53). In Revelations 8: 6-13 seven angels were loosed to execute judgment in the earth, "And I beheld, and heard an angel flying through the midst of heaven, saying with a loud voice, Woe, woe, woe, to the inhabitants of the earth by reason of the other voices of the trumpet of the three angels, which are yet to sound." Also in Genesis 18:20 and 19:13 the Angels came to destroy Sodom and Gomorrah "And the Lord said, Because the cry of Sodom and Gomorrah is great, and because their sin is very grievous." "For we will destroy this place, because the cry of them is waxen great before the face of the Lord; and the Lord has sent us to destroy it." Herod, the king, in Acts 12: 21-23 was smote by an angel:

"And upon a set day Herod, arrayed in royal apparel, sat upon his throne, and made an oration unto them. And the people gave a shout, saying, it is the voice of a god and not a man. And

immediately the angel of the Lord smote him, because he gave not God the glory: and he was eaten of worms, and gave up the ghost."

As noted in the examples above the Lord has made provisions for the believer to utilize angels in prayer. I challenge you to begin to make a conscious effort from this day forward to commission the angels assigned to your life to assist you in prayer. Remember the angels have been sent forth to minister to them who shall be heirs of salvation (Hebrews 1:14), and that is you and me. Hallelujah!

THE BLOOD OF JESUS

The blood of Jesus Christ is definitely a key in prayer. The Bible tells us in Hebrews 9: 22 that without the shedding of blood there is no remission of sin. What does this really mean? Without Jesus willingly going to the cross, dying, shedding His blood, we would all be sinners doomed to eternal death. But because of the blood of Jesus we are no longer doomed and now have a right to eternal life if we accept Jesus as Lord Savior. Because the blood of Jesus was shed at the cross we no longer have to stand on our own goodness but rather we look to the blood of Jesus which is pure, without blemish.

Isaiah 64: 6
"But we are all as an unclean thing, and all our righteousness are as filthy rags…"

In the Old Testament the Priest had to offer a sacrificial unblemished lamb to God for the remissions of the people's sins but in the New Testament Jesus became that lamb ("Behold the Lamb of God that taketh away the sin of the world" John 1: 29).

Hebrews 9: 12-14

9: 12 "Neither by the blood of goats and calves, but by his own blood he entered in once into the holy place, having obtained eternal redemption for us.

9: 13 "For if the blood of bulls and of goats, and the ashes of a heifer sprinkling the unclean, sanctifieth the purifying of the flesh:

9:14 "How much more shall the blood of Christ, who through the eternal Spirit offered himself without spot to God, purge your conscience from dead works to serve the Living God.

When Jesus went to the cross His blood was shed in at least seven places from His body. Many scholars have discussed, in detail, the significance of the seven locations, for this study we will focus mainly on the power that is in the blood. The power of the blood causes us to appear clean before our heavenly Father. The blood of Jesus gives us the right to enter boldly to the throne of grace and obtain mercy and find grace to help in time of need.

Hebrews 4: 16

"Let us therefore come boldly unto the throne of grace, that we may obtain mercy, and find grace to help in time of need."

Hebrews 10: 19

"Having therefore, brethren, boldness to enter into the holiest by the blood of Jesus."

The blood of Jesus gives us confidence to come boldly before God's presence. Why? Because we understand when we come with the Blood of Jesus we don't have to come on our own merits but rather on the finished work of the cross. We must understand that when we plead the Blood of Jesus the Father sees Jesus, He sees the pureness of Jesus and He answers accordingly. This is not by any means to imply that the Father does not know the difference but rather the blood is like a stamp of approval in the spirit, an okay, a green light. To the Devil, the Blood is terror because it reminds him of his defeat at the cross. It also reminds the Devil that he can't get to whatever is covered in the blood.

The best natural example I can think of is like when there is an outbreak, quarantine, and all the people that come to help have on body suits, their heads and faces are totally covered. With their armor on, there is absolutely no way that the outbreak or virus can get to them, they are totally protected, immune from the effects of the outbreak. In like manner when we pray and cover ourselves and situations with the Blood of Jesus we become immune to the effects of the Devil's attack.

There are times when I pray that I just call on the name of the Blood of Jesus. Why would I do that? The bible says that the Blood of Jesus speaks better things than the blood of Abel.

Hebrews 12: 24
"And to Jesus the mediator of the new covenant, and to the blood of sprinkling, that speaketh better things than that of Abel."

You may ask, what does that mean? Well, in Genesis 3: we note that the blood of Abel cried out for vengeance when he was murdered by his brother Cain.

Genesis 4: 9-10
4: 9 "And the Lord said unto Cain, "Where is Abel thy brother? And he said, "I know not: Am I my brother's keeper?"
4:10 "And he said, What has thou done? The voice of thy brother's blood crieth unto me from the grave."

But in Hebrews the scripture says that Jesus Blood speaks better things. Because Jesus Bloods says that we are guiltless because He already paid the price. Jesus Blood cries out "have mercy because I took on their sins at the cross, because my Blood was shed on their behalf," and therefore God is no longer angry with us. If we only understood the power of the blood, we would plead the Blood of Jesus around our bodies, our homes, our jobs for divine protection. In Exodus the children of Israel were directed by God to apply the blood on the door post of their homes and that the destroyer, the death angel would pass over their homes.

Exodus 12: 7, 12-13

12:7 "And they shall take of the blood, and strike it on the two side posts and on the upper door post of the houses, wherein they shall eat it."

12: 12 "For I will pass through the land of Egypt this night, and will smite all the firstborn in the land of Egypt, both man and beast; and against all the gods of Egypt I will execute judgment: "I am the Lord."

12: 13 "And the blood shall be to you for a token upon the houses where ye are: and when I see the blood I will pass over you, and the plague shall not be upon you to destroy you, when I smite the land of Egypt."

When the children of Israel obeyed, although all the other first born in that area died, the children of Israel, where the blood had been applied, lived. Praise God! The Devil, the destroyer, the death angel can not cross the blood line. When we apply the Blood of Jesus by speaking the Word, Satan and his demons tremble. They tremble because they were there when Jesus was crucified; they saw the Blood of Jesus and the effects of what the shedding of Jesus Blood did. The spiritual world trembles when you pray and speak the blood of Jesus. The Blood of Jesus gives us a right to access the throne of God. It protects us from unforeseen harm. It blocks the assignments of the enemy. Therefore, when you pray apply the blood of Jesus to your circumstances and watch as things began to happen, to turn to your advantage. You will begin to receive answers to your prayers quicker. The Blood of Jesus will cover and protect you from the attacks and the opposition of the enemy against your prayers. Below is a prayer that can be prayed about the Blood of Jesus:

PRAYER

Father, I thank you that Jesus shed His Blood on the cross for my sins and now I am clean and guiltless before you. I boldly approach your throne to obtain grace and mercy to help in my time of need. You said to the children of Israel that they should plead the blood of goats and lambs on the door post and the death angel would pass over. How much more will the Blood of Jesus protect me from all hurt, harm and danger and I thank you Father for the privilege to use the Blood, to speak into and for my life. Thank you that the Blood is speaking mercy instead of judgment for my life. Because of Your Son Jesus Blood demons tremble and run in terror when they hear me speak the Blood of Jesus. Therefore, Lord I ask that you begin to teach me, to train me, to open my eyes to the benefit of using the Blood of Jesus in prayer. Amen.

TIMING OF GOD

God has a perfect plan for all creation and we as individuals all fit into that plan. Within God's perfect plan there is a perfect timing for manifestation of all prayer. The timing of God is crucial in answered prayer. The scripture says in Ecclesiastes 3:1 "To every thing there is a season, and a time to every purpose under the heaven" and Daniel 2:21 say's "And he changeth the times and seasons…" Because God is omniscient, He knows everything, He knows the perfect season and timing to answer our prayers. There may be times that we ask for things that we are not really ready for. For example, a parent would not give a car to a 12 year old, although the child greatly desires the car and although the parent may have the means to provide the car. First, it is illegal for a 12 year-old to drive a car and secondly, the child's ability to quickly judge and make decisions usually is not sharp enough at 12 to handle the responsibility of driving a car, and would consequently put the child at risk of being hurt. God is so wise that He would not give us something that we desire if He knows it will bring harm or destruction to us.

The children in the Old Testament prayed and looked diligently for the coming Messiah. In Malachi the scripture makes reference to the coming messiah "Behold I will send my messenger, and he shall prepare the way before me: and the Lord, whom ye seek, shall suddenly come to his temple, even the messenger of the covenant, whom ye delight in: behold, he shall come, saith the Lord of hosts." God was speaking of John the Baptist as His messenger and the Lord Jesus Christ as the messenger of the covenant, but note that it was over 400 years from the time of that scripture that it was fulfilled in Mark 1:2 when John the Baptist even showed up on the scene. In Luke 4: 18-19 Jesus made reference to himself as the Messiah and that the Spirit of the Lord was upon him:

> *"The Spirit of the Lord is upon me, because he hath anointed me to preach the gospel to the brokenhearted, to preach deliverance to the captives, and recovery of sight to the blind, to set at liberty them that are bruised. To preach the acceptable year of the Lord."*

The Lord Jesus goes on to say in verse 21 "This day is this Scripture fulfilled in your ears." This scripture had been prophesied hundreds of years ago by the Prophet Isaiah, but it did not come to pass until there in Luke chapter 4. The scripture often refers to the statement in the "fullness of time" When Jesus stood and read that scripture it was the fullness of time. We also see in Exodus that the King of Egypt had given the children of Israel a hard time for many years and although they had prayed and sought the Lord, their prayers had not been answered. In Exodus 2:23-24 the Lord answered their prayers but there was a process of time that had to occur first "And it came to pass in process of time that the king of Egypt died: and the children of Israel sighed by reason of the bondage, and they cried and their cry came up unto God by reason of the bondage, and God heard their groaning and God remembered his covenant with Abraham, with Isaac, and with Jacob." God had heard the prayers of the children but the king's heart was hardened toward God. Because of the loving kindness and mercy of the Father, He sometimes will allow time for people to repent before he judges the situation or answers the prayer when others are in involved in your prayer request. When the disciples inquired of Jesus before his final departure in Acts if this was the time that He would restore again the kingdom to Israel, Jesus replied "It is not for you to know the times or the seasons, which the Father has put in his own power." We don't always know the perfect timing of God, but our job is to remain in faith, trusting God and looking diligently to Him for the answer. The true test of our faith is when we continue to trust and believe God in the face of adversity and boldly state and believe, "if God said it, I believe it" and trust God to bring the answer to pass.

SCRIPTURE REFERENCE:

Isaiah 55:10-11	Luke 12:32
John 16: 7, 13, 23-24	Psalm 103:20, 21
Acts 12: 6-8, 11-16	Joshua 2:4
Psalm 37:4	Luke 1:11, 13, 30,31
Hebrew 7:25, 10:12, 11: 1,6, 13:8	Hebrew 1: 14
Acts 5: 19	Daniel 10:12-13
Psalm 21:2	Colossians 1: 15-16
Mark 9:23	Revelation 8:6-13
Acts 12:21-23	Revelations 12:7
Proverbs 10:24	John 1:1-3
Matthew 17:20	Genesis 4:24
Matthew 4:11	Jude 1:9
John 6:63	John 14:13-14, 26
Romans 4:3, 20, 21	Matthew 4:11
Matthew 26:53	Exodus 2:23-24

CHAPTER QUESTIONS

1. Name three of the key components to answered prayer.

    _____

    _____

2. Which component of prayer is mainly the believer's responsibility?

    _____

    _____

3. Which component of prayer is most under utilized?

    _____

    _____

4. Name at least two scriptural ways angels may be used in prayer.

    _____

    _____

5. In scripture the reference to the "Fullness of Time" refers to which of the components of answers to prayer.

    _____

    _____

"…And Thine Ears Shall Hear a Word Behind Thee Saying, This is the Way Walk Ye in it."

ISAIAH 30:21

CHAPTER 3

Answered Prayer in the Bible

As we look through the Word of God there are several examples of God answering the prayers of His saints. Some prayers were answered immediately, a miracle; yet others in stages and some were answered in the "fullness of time" as we mentioned earlier. In this next chapter we will focus on some of these examples of answered prayer. As we study these examples our faith will be encouraged realizing that the scripture notes, "Now all these things happened unto them for examples: and they are written for our admonition, upon whom the ends of the world are come" (I Corinthians 10:11). In the "King James Lexical Aids to the New Testament" the word "admonition" is translated, Nouthesis. "Nouthesis is the training by a word of encouragement when it proves sufficient, but also by a word of remonstrance, reproof, as required." The following examples of answered prayer will be admonition or will encourage you that if God answered their prayer that He can and will answer yours. As we take a look at a few men and women of faith who stood strong and received answers to their prayers we will find strength and confidence to stand in prayer knowing that God is "the same Yesterday, and Today and forever, Hebrews 13:8."

HANNAH

The first person of faith that we will look at is Hannah found in I Samuel

1& 2.   Hannah had a desperate situation; she was married and she was barren. Her husband, Elkanah had two wives. His second wife's name was Peninnah, and she had children. Unfortunately Peninnah "also provoked her (Hannah) sore, for to make her fret because the Lord had shut up her womb." However Peninnah failed to note the favor of the Lord on Hannah's life, "But unto Hannah he gave a worthy portion; for he loved Hannah." In Hannah's weeping and sorrow she decided to pray a prayer of petition to the only God who has authority to open or close the womb. In I Samuel 1:11 the scripture notes that Hannah prayed this prayer "…Oh Lord of Host, If thou wilt indeed look on the afflictions of thine handmaiden, and remember me, and not forget thine handmaid, but will give unto thine handmaiden a man child, then I will give him unto the Lord all the days of his life, and there shall no razor come upon his head." We see in her prayer that she address the Lord in adoration first "Oh Lord of Host." She then begins to petition the Lord in prayer. Notice that Hannah's prayer was very specific, she not only wanted a child, but she wanted a "man child." She then does an amazing thing; she makes a vow; and the very child that she is praying for she commits back to the Lord. In verse 19 the Lord answers her prayer, "And they rose up in the morning early, and worshiped before the Lord, and returned, and came to their house to Ramah: and Elkanah knew Hannah his wife; and the Lord remembered her." "Wherefore it came to pass, when the time was come about after Hannah had conceived, that she bare a son, and called his name Samuel, saying, Because I have asked him of the Lord." It appears here that the Lord answered Hannah's prayer the very next day. Hannah also kept her end of the deal; after the "male child" was weaned she took him up to the priest. Note in the following verses 26-28; "And she said, Oh my Lord, as thy soul liveth, my lord, I am the woman that stood by thee here, praying unto the Lord. For this child I prayed; and the Lord hath given me my petition which I asked of him. Therefore also I have lent him to the Lord; and as long as he liveth he shall be lent to the Lord. And he worshiped the Lord there." Here we see that Hannah actually left her son with Eli the Priest. The very child that she had prayed and asked the Lord for, she was also willing to give him back to the Lord. The bible says she did it with joy. "And Hannah prayed, and said; My heart rejoiceth in the Lord, mine horn is exalted in the Lord: my mouth is enlarged over mine enemies; because I rejoice in thy salvation. There is none holy as the Lord; for there is none beside the: neither is there any rock like our God." However God can never be out done; according to the Word of God in Luke 6:38, "Give and it shall be given unto thee." Hannah kept her end of the bargain but look at what God did for her obedience in I Samuel 2: 21 "And the Lord visited Hannah, so that she conceived, and bare three sons and two daughters." The story of Hannah is an example of the Lord gloriously answering the prayers of His saints. Hannah asked for one child and the Lord gave her five more. We know and see according to scripture that the Lord is "able to do exceedingly, abundantly, above all that we ask or think, according to the power that worketh in us" (Ephesians 3:20).

Several years ago a close family member of mine had been told for years that she would never have children because of a problem with her uterus. She called me one day and asked if I would pray for her to have a baby. She talked about how much she really wanted a baby but, the doctors had told her she could not have children. We talked for a while about what the Word of God says and then I began to pray, in Jesus name, that the God that created all wombs would heal and open her womb. In less than 2 months she was pregnant and today she has two healthy baby girls. Praise the Lord! God also opened the womb of another young lady that is mentioned as a testimony in the back of this book. God not only open her womb but He blessed her with three at one time. How great is our God! He not only opened Hannah's womb in the Old Testament but, He is still in the business of opening wombs. Remember He is the same yesterday and today and forever (Hebrews 13:8).

ABRAHAM

Abraham is the next person of prayer that we will study. In Genesis 18 Abraham gives us a beautiful example of Intercessory Prayer. In Intercessory Prayer we know that prayer is made on behalf of another's sin or wrong to avert the judgment of God. According to Ezekiel 22:30, God often looks for a man to stand in the gap, to prevent judgment, "And I sought for a man among them that should make up the hedge, and stand in the gap before me for the land, that I should not destroy it: but I found none." In Genesis 18:20-21 the sins of Sodom and Gomorrah came up before the Lord:

> *"And the Lord said, Because the cry of Sodom and Gomorrah is great; and because their sin is very grievous; I will go down now, and see whether they have done altogether according to the cry of it, which is come unto me; and if not I will know."*

Abraham had a great concern for the city of Sodom and Gomorrah because his nephew Lot and Lot's family lived in that city. God had alerted Abraham, His Prophet, prior to executing judgement, "And the Lord said, Shall I hide from Abraham that thing which I do." We see in Amos 3:7 that "Surely the Lord God will do nothing but he revealeth his secret unto his servants the prophets." It seems here that the Lord wanted to spare Lot and his family, but He needed an Intercessor to pray. Abraham quickly stepped up to the plate to intercede in verse 23, "And Abraham drew near, and said, Wilt thou also destroy the righteous with the wicked?" Abraham had an intimate relationship with God and although he asked this question he knew the answer and he knew God knew, but he continued his plea with God to save his family. Abraham first asked if there be fifty righteous found will God spare the city and finally ends his pray in verse 32, "And he said, Oh let not the Lord be angry, and I will speak yet but this once: Peradventure ten shall be found there. And he said I will not destroy it for ten's sake." In Genesis 19:12 we see the Lord sending angels to deliver Lot and his family,

"And the men said unto Lot, hast thou here any besides? Son in law, and thy sons, and thy daughters, and whatsoever thou hast in the city, bring them out of this place: For we will destroy this place, because the cry of them is waxen great before the face of the Lord; and the Lord hath sent us to destroy it."

We see the power of Abraham's prayer on behalf of Lot in Genesis 19:22 when the angel that came to destroy the city said "Haste thee, escape thither; for I cannot do anything till thou be come thither." In other words the prayer of Abraham bound the angel; destruction could not occur until Lot was delivered. God heard and answered the prayer of His servant Abraham, "And it came to pass, when God destroyed the cities of the plain, that God remembered Abraham, and sent Lot out of the midst of the overthrow, when he overthrew the cities in which Lot dwelt." God is faithful to hear and answer the prayers of the righteous to avert judgment. It is amazing that God has extended such authority to His children through prayer. We can actually pray a prayer according to God's will and prevent danger or harm from overcoming our loved ones. Therefore, let us be mindful daily of the authority that we have received and use it to stop the plan of the Devil in our lives and the lives of others.

ELIJAH

Elijah was a great man of faith who prayed a Prayer of Faith that stopped the rain for three years. In James 5:17:

"Elias was a man subject to like passions as we are, and he prayed earnestly that it might not rain: and it rained not on the earth by the space of three years and six months. And he prayed again, and the heaven gave rain, and the earth brought forth her fruit."

In I Kings 17:1 Elijah in faith spoke a word of prayer to Ahab "As the Lord God of Israel liveth, before whom I stand, there shall not be dew nor rain these years, but according to my word." That was a strong statement of faith but, Elijah knew his God "Behold, I am the Lord, the God of all flesh: is there any thing too hard for me?" (Jeremiah 32:27). God answered Elijah's prayer. In I King 18:1 we see the answer, "And it came to pass after many days, that the word of the Lord came to Elijah in the third year, saying, Go, show thyself unto Ahab: and I will send rain upon the earth." In I Kings 18:41-44 we see that Elijah did not stop praying until he saw the full manifestation of his prayer, "And Elijah said unto Ahab, get thee up, eat and drink; for there is a sound of an abundance of rain." Elijah began to confess the answer to his prayer even before he saw the manifestation. He continues in prayer in verse 42:

"...And Elijah went up to the top of Carmel; and he cast himself down upon the earth, and put his face between his knee, and said to his servant, Go up now, look toward the sea. And he went up, and looked, and said, There is nothing. And he said, Go again seven times. And it came to pass at the seventh time, that he said, Behold, there ariseth a little cloud out of the sea, like a man's hand. And he said, Go up, say unto Ahab, Prepare thy chariot, and get thee down, that the rain stop thee not. And it came to pass in the mean while, that the heaven was black with clouds and wind, and there was a great rain."

Again we see that God answers the prayers of His saints. Elijah and the servants of God in the Old Testament only had the spirit of the Lord upon them. How blessed we are today as Christians who have the spirit of the Lord not only on us but He lives within us. Therefore, if Elijah could pray a prayer to withhold and release rain, at the direction of the Lord, how much more can we pray and expect answers.

SOLOMON

Solomon prayed the prayer of supplication when he was building the temple of the Lord in I Kings 8:22-30. Solomon, as king, petitioned the throne of God for himself and the people of God, "And Solomon stood before the altar of the lord in the presence of all the congregation of Israel, and spread forth his hands toward heaven: and he said, Lord God of Israel, there is no God like thee, in heaven above, or on earth beneath, who keepest covenant and mercy with thy servants that walk before thee with all their heart: Who hast kept with thy servant David my father that thou promisedst him: thou spakest also with thy mouth; and hast fulfilled it with thine hand, as it is this day. Therefore now, Lord God of Israel, keep with thy servant David that thou promisedst him, saying, There shall not fail thee a man in my sight to sit on the throne of Israel; so that thy children take heed to their way, that they walk before me as thou hast walked before me. And now, O God of Israel, let thy word, I pray thee, be verified, which thou spakest unto thy servant David my father. But will God indeed dwell on the earth? Behold, the heaven and heaven of heavens cannot contain thee; how much less this house that I have builded? Yet have thou respect unto the prayer of thy servant, and to his supplication, Oh Lord my God, to hearken unto the cry and to the prayer, which thy servant prayeth before thee today. That my eyes may be open toward this house night and day, even toward the place of which thou hast said, "My name shall be there: that thou mayest hearken unto the prayer which thy servant shall make toward this place. And hearken thou to the supplication of thy servant, and of thy people Israel, when they shall pray toward this place: and hear thou in heaven thy dwelling place: and when thou hearest, forgive." Solomon continued on in prayer throughout the entire eighth chapter of I King. We see as we closely examine this prayer that it is actually a corporate prayer lead by Solomon the King. In I Kings 9:3-4 God answers the prayer of Solomon, "And the Lord said unto him, I have heard thy prayer and thy supplication, that thou hast made before me; I have hallowed this house, which thou hast built, to put my name there forever; and mine eyes and mine heart shall be there perpetually. And if thou wilt walk before me, as David thy father walked, in integrity of heart, and in uprightness, to do according to all that I have commanded thee, and wilt keep my statutes and my judgments: Then I will establish the throne of thy kingdom upon Israel forever." God did answer Solomon's prayer but He gave him the criteria for this prayer to be continually fulfilled. Often the Lord requires obedience to His instructions to receive the full manifestation of the prayer request.

DANIEL

Daniel was a great man of prayer who prayed a prayer of Intercession on behalf of himself and the children of Israel. The Lord did answer his prayer by sending an angel in Daniel 9: 3-23 and chapter 10. Daniel starts off by praying in verse 3, "and I set my face to the Lord God to seek by prayer and supplication, and fasting, and sackcloth, and ashes and ends in verse 21-23. Daniel 9:21 "Yea, whiles I was speaking in prayer, even the man Gabriel, whom I had seen in the vision at the beginning, being caused to fly swiftly, touched me about the time of the evening oblation. We see here in verse 21 that God sent an angel in response to Daniel's prayer "At the beginning of thy supplications the commandment came forth, and I am come to show thee; for thou art greatly beloved; therefore understand the matter, and consider the vision." How powerful it is to consider that God could send an angel to assist in bringing answers to our prayer as He did for Daniel in the Old Testament.

NEW TESTAMENT ANSWERED PRAYERS

Peter and John in Acts chapter 3 is an example of God answering prayer in the New Testament

"Now Peter and John went up together into the temple at the hour prayer, being the ninth hour. And a certain man lame from his mother's womb was carried, whom they laid daily at the gate of the temple which is called Beautiful, to ask alms of them that entered into the temple; Who seeing Peter and John about to go into the temple asked an alms. And Peter, fastening his eyes upon him with John, said, Look on us. And he gave heed unto them, expecting to receive something of them. Then Peter said, Silver and gold have I none; but such as I have give I thee: In the name of Jesus Christ of Nazareth rise up and walk. And he took him by the right hand, and lifted him up: and immediately his feet and ankle bones received strength. And he leaping up stood, and walked, and entered with them into the temple, walking, and leaping, and praising God."

Here we see God answering the prayer of faith prayed by Peter and John along with the gift of faith in operation. After this miracle occurred the religious leaders became upset and threaten Peter and John that they should no longer teach in Jesus name. But notice how Peter and John prayed, "And now Lord, behold their threatenings: and grant unto thy servants, that with all boldness they may speak thy word, By stretching forth thine hand to heal; and that signs and wonders may be done by the name of thy holy child Jesus." Peter and John prayed a bold prayer of faith and notice what happened immediately in verse 31, "And when they had prayed, the place was shaken where they were assembled together; and they were all filled with the Holy Ghost, and they spake the word of God with boldness."

Again in Acts chapter 16 we note Paul and Silas getting immediate answers to their prayers. In verse 25 the bible says "And at midnight Paul and Silas prayed and sang praises unto God: and the prisoners heard them, and suddenly there was a great earthquake, so that the foundations of the prison were shaken: and immediately all the doors were opened, and every one's bands were loosed." Thank God that we can be assured that God does not change if He did it before He can do it again because He is not a respecter of persons. Throughout the Bible, Old Testament and New, there are numerous examples of God answering prayer.

STAGES OF RECEIVING ANSWERED PRAYER

In this section we will look at least three (3) stages which are necessary to obtain answers to prayers. The stages are as follows:

1. A prayer request that is inspired by God
2. Confession
3. Manifestation

In the first stage we must be certain that the prayer is scripturally based and God inspired. In Genesis 1:1 we note "In the beginning God created the heaven and the earth." At the very beginning in scripture we see that God started by creating; the heaven and earth was something God wanted. In Genesis 1:2 we see that "the earth was without form, and void." Likewise when we have a prayer request it is indeed void and without form; in other words there is nothing seen or tangibly present, only the thought or request. In requesting something in prayer we must first be sure that it is the will of God that it is something God wants. The prayer must be first inspired, created or originate from God not man or human inspired. This step is extremely important. Is it part of God's plan? Or did you come up with it? The only way to know for sure is through intimacy with God. For example the will of God concerning healing is according to III John 1:2 "Beloved I wish above all things that thou mayest prosper and be in health, even as though soul prospereth." Therefore according to this scripture we know that it is the will of the Lord for us to be healed. But, what if we decide that we will be healed by an instant miracle? Because we know the will of the Lord on the subject does not mean that we automatically know the will of the Lord for our individual situations or the way of escape He has designed for our lives. In the instance of healing there are several methods that God may choose (i.e., miracle, confessing and walking it out by faith, medication or even surgery). However, you must seek the face of the Lord; spend time in fellowship, to determine what the will of the Lord is concerning you for healing. The scripture in James 4:3 says "Ye ask, and receive not, because ye ask amiss, that ye may consume it upon your lusts." If the request or prayer is because we observed that God gave something to someone and we want it or, we want to tell God how to do a thing, contrary to the way He has chosen, this is asking amiss. Be certain that if our prayer request is amiss that we will not get the answer. In I John 5:14-15 the scripture say's, "And this is the confidence that we have in him, that, if we ask any thing according to his will, he heareth us: And if we know that he hear us whatsoever we ask, we know that we have the petitions that we desired of him. When we ask God in prayer, according to his will, we can pray in confidence knowing that he will surely hear and answer our prayers.

Secondly if God created or originated the request and we have confidence from God that it is His timing, then the next stage is to speak or confess over the thing what God has already said about it (call those things that be not as though they were). When God told Abram that He was going to make him a father of many nations in Genesis 17:5, God didn't wait until it completely manifested. God changed his name at the time He told him and began to call him Abraham from that day forward ("Neither shall thy name any more be called Abram, but thy name shall be Abraham: for a father of many nations have I made thee"). The scripture in Romans 4:12 refers to God as He "who quickeneth the dead, and calleth those things which be not as though they were." If our Father in heaven calls those things that be not as though they already are, how much more should we as His children do the same. Also in Hebrews 11:3 we note that the worlds were actually created by the spoken Word of God. Everything that God wanted in the world He spoke it into existence (Genesis 1).

My husband and I had lived in our last home for about 5 years when the Lord began to deal with us about buying a new home. When the Lord put the idea in our hearts there was nothing in the natural that indicated that it was God's timing. We were in debt, and about three months behind on our present note. Nevertheless, by faith, we began to believe God for a new home. As we began to look at new homes the area that we thought God was leading us in was almost three times the size of the home that we lived in. Quite honestly we had never really been in a home of the size we were looking at. Our Pastor would always tell the congregation to get out the box, get out of the comfort zone. He suggested that on Sunday evenings we should drive into other neighborhoods and get the feel of the atmosphere. Pastor would say just go looking and walk around in some of those big houses to get use to it. Well, we did and wow it was really different at first. We soon became very comfortable with the larger homes and our hearts were ready to believe God. After we agreed upon a home that we liked I got a picture of the home and put it in my prayer folder. Everyday we would thank God for our new home. In spite of our natural financial situation we trusted God. All you need is a Word from God and that one Word can defy every natural circumstance. We laid hands on the home and we sowed seeds for the home. Remember it is not always the size of your seed but the obedience. We sowed $3.50 seed for a $350,000 home. At the time we only had that amount and God honored our faith. Although we had a lot of financial difficulties we were committed to tithing and giving to our church. Before we walked into our miracle home we believed and confessed for almost two years. During that time the actual home we believed for was sold and someone else moved in. We were devastated. But we didn't give up. Almost two years to the day we started believing God for a new home we found the house God had for us. I remember being confused and upset when the other house was sold. I know God said He had a house

for us but, I didn't understand how someone else could move in. The
same principle applied as with the job I believed for; if I didn't get
the house, it wasn't really mine. The devil can't block what is really
yours. When we found the home it was in another part of the city
but it was almost identical to the home we had believed for except
it was on more property and several thousands dollars less. It was
so amazing because when we found it, it had been built two years
prior and lived in for a month. The house was built by a builder for
himself but his partner got in a bad business deal and the company
went under. So the house was just sitting and it needed to be sold
in a hurry. At the same time God spoke to us about a new home, He
had it built but, it took us two years to find it. Sometimes we think
God has not answered our prayers but it is really that we are at the
wrong location or address to receive the delivery.

The third and final stage to receiving answered prayer is manifestation. First we know that it is God's will, that it is part of His plan for our lives and we are assured that it is His timing and we have spoken or confessed His word concerning it. Next, the manifestation occurs suddenly (a miracle) or most often in stages as in Mark 4:26-29, first the blade, then the ear, after that the full corn in the ear ("So is the kingdom of God, as if a man should cast seed into the ground; and should sleep, and rise night and day, and the seed should spring and grow up, he knoweth not how. For the earth bringeth forth fruit of herself; first the blade, then the ear, after that the full corn in the ear.") As we wait in this final stage for the full manifestation, we should praise God as if it is already done. Remember these stages can occur immediately, a miracle, or it could take months or even years to manifest. But we must remain steadfast, unmovable realizing that if He promised He will bring it to pass and that according to Numbers 23:19,

"God is not a man, that he should lie; neither the son of man, that
he should repent: hath he said, and shall he not do it? Or hath he

spoken, and shall he not make it good?"

Once you have heard God and have the scripture to back you up, don't give up until you get the full manifestation and you too can be entered into the "Faith Hall of Fame," where men and women believed God even unto death (Hebrews 11).

SCRIPTURE REFERENCE:

I Corinthians 10:11	Ezekiel 22:30
Jeremiah 32:27	I John 5: 14-15
Hebrews 11:17-40, 13:8	Genesis 18: 20-21
I King 8: 22-30	Romans 4:12
I Samuel 1:11, 26-28	Genesis 19:12, 22
Daniel 9: 3-23	Genesis 17:5
Luke 6:38	Amos 3:7
Genesis 1: 1, 2	Mark 4: 26 - 29
Ephesians 3:20	James 5:17
III John 1: 2	I Kings 17:1, 18:1, 41-44

CHAPTER QUESTIONS

1. Who in scripture prayed a prayer that stopped the judgment of God from coming on his nephew and family?

    _____

    _____

2. Which prophet prayed a prayer that caused the rains to be released after 3 years of drought?

    _____

    _____

3. Who prayed a prayer that God heard immediately but needed the assistance of an angel to get the full breakthrough?

    _____

    _____

4. Name the two apostles who prayed and were delivered from jail.

    _____

    _____

I am not against you,
I am for you.
I do not curse you,
I bless you
I do not pull you,
I lead you...

"Be Still, and Know That I am God"
PSALM 46:10

CHAPTER 4

<hr>

Hindrances to Answered Prayer

In the past chapters we discussed some of the key components and stages to answered prayer and looked at some examples in the Word of God of answered prayer. In this chapter we will look at some things which may cause a person's prayers not to be answered. For the purpose of this study manual we will focus on six areas that will definitely hinder prayer. We will discuss each of the following in detail:

1. Sin
   a. Pride
   b. An Unforgiving Heart (not walking in love)
2. Unbelief
3. Fear
4. Asking amiss
5. Wavering
6. Wrong season or timing

SIN

The first hindrance that we will look at is sin in general. The Bible says, "If I regard iniquity in my heart, the Lord will not hear me" Psalm 66:18. According to the scripture if there is iniquity in our hearts the Lord is not willing to hear our prayers. Therefore, as a person of prayer, one of the very first things that we must do is to make sure there is no sin in our life by coming before the Lord with a repentant heart. We must first seek the Lord in Prayer for forgiveness of all our sins, those that we know about and those that we are not aware of. We must inquire of the Lord to show us our own heart. For the scripture says that "For from within, out of the heart of men, proceed evil thoughts, adulteries, fornications, murders, thefts, covetousness, wickedness, deceit, lasciviousness, an evil eye, blasphemy, pride, foolishness: all these evil things come from within and defile a man." Mark 7:21-23. All of these things come from within a man to defile him.

There was a time in my life when it seemed that the presence of God had left me. It was as though my prayers were hitting a brick wall. As I began to earnestly pray and ask God what was going on, He revealed that I had unforgiveness in my heart toward my husband. My husband and I have a beautiful relationship but, there are always opportunities for disagreement in marriage. Usually I am quick to repent when we have a disagreement but, this time somehow it slipped by. Remember the scripture says if I regard iniquity in my heart the Lord will not hear my prayers. The hidden sin of unforgiveness had crept in my heart and had hindered my prayers. Additionally, the Lord revealed to me that the strife and unforgiveness was not just against any man but, against the authority in my home. I realized immediately the seriousness of the sin and the devastating effects it could have on my life by being cut off from my spiritual authority and natural authority. I repented quickly to God and my husband. As soon as I repented I could sense the tangible presence of God return and my prayers were answered again. I thank God for the Holy Ghost that leads us into all truth.

As a Believer it is important to "Keep thy heart with all diligence: for out of it are the issues of life." It is the responsibility of the Believer to keep or guard his/her own heart. We must continually check our hearts to make sure it remains pure and clean before the Lord. Matthew 5:8 says "blessed are the pure in heart: for they shall see God." Also in Psalm 15: 1-5 David, the Psalmist, ask a very important question of the Lord, "Lord, who shall abide in thy tabernacle? Who shall dwell in thy holy hill?" David wanted to know who was able to come before God's throne. The Lord's answer was very specific:

"He that walketh uprightly, and worketh righteousness, and speaketh the truth in his heart. He that backbiteth not with his tongue, nor doeth evil to his neighbor, nor taketh up a reproach against his neighbor. In whose eyes a vile person is contemned: but he honoreth them that fear the Lord. He that sweareth to his own hurt and changeth not. He that putteth not out his money to usury, nor taketh reward against the innocent."

According to these scriptures there are certain requirements of a person of prayer before they can gain the full attention of the Almighty God. Again we see in I John 3:22 "And whatsoever we ask we receive of him, because we keep his commandments, and do those things that are pleasing in his sight." Of course we see that we must keep his commandments and one of the things that is pleasing in God's sight is faith. Hebrews 11:6 says "But without faith it is impossible to please him: for he that cometh to God must believe that he is, and that he is a rewarder of them that diligently seek him." It is always important to live a repentant lifestyle, but it is of utmost importance in the ministry of prayer. If you are aware of any hidden sin in your life that the Holy Ghost has dealt with you about in the past, now is the time to get it right. Always remember, in prayer holiness is power. When you are walking in the Word to the best of your knowledge and maintain a repentant heart the devil will recognize your authority and realizes that he must obey your prayers. Otherwise, if there is hidden sin in your life the devil knows it and you will not have the same authority in the spirit and your prayers will be ineffective. Scripturally there are many sins that can hinder prayer but for the purpose of this manual we will focus on a few common sins that can hinder the effectiveness of a person of prayer such as, pride and an unforgiving heart.

Pride

In Proverbs 6:17 God named six things that He hated and the very first thing on the list is "a proud look" or pride. My Pastor frequently says that he believes God lists pride first because it is the sin that is most like Satan. Pride takes God's credit. Pride says, "I don't need God," "I can do it all by myself," "I can lead my self," "I know the way." The scripture also says in Proverb 16:18, "Pride goeth before destruction and a haughty spirit before a fall." The spirit of pride blinds us to our own insufficiency; it is probably the most deadly spirit or sin because it deceives us into thinking we are right and that we have no faults. For a person of prayer this should be a flashing red light when we began to think we have arrived, to think that no one can instruct us, to feel that we have all the right answers and to think that we are the only ones that can pray or that can hear God. We must continually check ourselves and when we even sense a trace of pride we should run to God in repentance. Remember the scripture says that our righteousness is as filthy rags (Isaiah 64:6). Without the righteousness of Christ we are nothing… a hopeless case. Pride is an insidious sin because it sneaks up on you and you don't even realize its there but everyone else does. The best example I can think of is like having a terrible body odor, although initially you may be the first to smell it, if you don't correct it you get used to the odor but it is the first thing that everybody else notices about you and they all are wondering why you don't smell it.

An Unforgiving Heart

As mentioned earlier it is imperative for the person of prayer to keep a clean heart. It is our responsibility to spend time daily before the Lord confessing our sin. According to the scripture in 1 John 1:9, "If we confess our sins, he is faithful and just to forgive us our sins, and to cleanse us from all unrighteousness." Another sin that the devil often uses to hinder prayer is the sin of unforgiveness. There are several references in the Bible that indicates that prayer will not be heard if there is an unforgiving heart or if there is an offense against your brethren. The scripture goes even further to say that we should get up from the altar and go and ask for forgiveness or get it right with our brother or sister and then come back to him and present our gift or prayer. The Father places great emphasis on forgiveness and not holding offense against our sister or brother. In I Corinthians 13, the chapter on love indicates, according to the Amplified version, in verses 5 and 6 that "love takes no account of the evil done to it, pays no attention to a suffered wrong." The Lord does not expect us to keep up with how many times our sister or brother hurts or offends us. But rather the Father expects us to forgive and release them as many times as necessary. In Matthew 18: 21-22 Peter asks the Lord an interesting question; note the answer Jesus gives him:

"Then came Peter to him, and said, Lord, how oft shall my brother sin against me, and I forgive him? Till seven times? Jesus saith unto him, I say not unto thee, until seven times: but until seventy times seven."

In this scripture there is great expectation of the Lord for us when it comes to forgiveness. According to scripture our Faith can't even work if we are not walking in love (Galatians 5:6 – "but faith which worketh by love"). Remember in John 3:16 that God so love the world that he gave his only begotten Son, that whosoever believeth in him should not perish, but have everlasting life." God the Father sent His only begotten son to die on the cross for a people that rejected and despised Him. Jesus' cross experience, death and resurrection is the foundation for Christianity. This is the greatest example of forgiveness, of love. In spite of how the religious leaders rejected

His only begotten Son, the Father yet gave his Son's life for us. Our Christian Faith and belief was founded on the principle of love. Therefore if God forgave us of our sins, totally, He expects us to do the same for our sisters and brothers. Jesus went on to say in scripture that if we have aught in our hearts and come to him in prayer that we should first go and get it right and then come back to him to pray. In other words it seems that God will not hear or is not willing to listen to us if we haven't forgiven someone.

> *Mark 11:24*
> *"Therefore I say unto you, what things so ever ye desire, when you pray, believe that ye receive, and ye shall have them. And when ye stand praying forgive, if ye have aught against any: that your Father also which is in heaven may forgive you your trespasses. But if ye do not forgive, neither will your Father which is in heaven forgive your trespasses."*

This scripture should be given great thought; The Father actually will not forgive us if we don't forgive others. We can definitely see here why an unforgiving heart would be a hindrance to our prayers. I once heard a well known minister make a profound statement, he said, "Unforgiveness is like looking at someone and wishing they would die, but you are the one that swallowed the rat poison." An unforgiving heart slowly eats away, destroys your spiritual life and your ability to fellowship and ability to hear from God.

UNBELIEF

In the scriptures, Romans 14:23, unbelief is considered as sin in the eyes of God "Whatever is not of faith is sin." In Galatians 6: 10 the scriptures indicates that we are of the "Household of Faith." In Romans 1:17 Paul quote Habakkuk 2:4 "The just shall live by faith." On numerous occasions in scripture we note that "the Lord could do no mighty works because of their unbelief" (Matthew 13:58, 17: 20, Mark 6:6, 16:14, Hebrew 3: 12, 19, 4: 6, 11). In Matthew the Lord's prayers were hindered because of the unbelief of the people, "And He did not many mighty works because of their unbelief." The writer of Hebrews takes it a step further in chapter 3:12 saying, "Take heed, brethren, lest there be in any of you an evil heart of unbelief." Here unbelief is referred to as evil. Again in Mark 6: 6, "and He marveled because of their unbelief." One of the first steps to receiving answers to our prayers is to believe that we receive the answer when we pray or ask.

FEAR

Fear is a very common hindrance in prayer and was personally my greatest challenge. Fear is the opposite or opposes faith. As we discussed in chapter II, faith is one of the keys to answered prayer. The enemy often uses the tactic of fear against a new person of prayer. If the spirit of fear is not dealt with it will become a stronghold in your life and will hinder your effectiveness in prayer. When the Lord first began to deal with me in prayer I had no problem praying alone with God but, I often became paralyzed in a group. The devil would frequently tell me that I was not called to prayer, that I did not know how to pray and that I certainly could not pray as effectively as the other seasoned prayer warriors I prayed with. My struggle with fear unfortunately lasted for years. You might ask "What happened to change this?" The thing that made the difference was just what we are discussing in this manual. I spent more time with God, in the Word, and in prayer. The more time I spent with God the more I became like His nature. Of course we all know that there is absolutely no fear in God. The more time I spent with God, the easier it became for me to talk, to commune with Him no matter who was present. In my relationship with the Lord I discovered that it did not matter if people thought I could pray but only that I could talk to my God and that He would hear me. After many years I realized that confidence in prayer comes from a solid relationship with the Lord. Think about the closest, most intimate relationship that you have… Are you afraid to talk to them? Are you shy and timid with them? The answer to all of these questions should be no. In like manner the closer the more intimate you become with the Lord, you will lose all fear, all intimidation and come boldly before His throne and find grace and mercy to help in a time of need. The scripture that I used most often to help me overcome fear is found in Proverbs 28:1, "The righteous are bold as a lion." There are many other scriptures that will help you overcome in this area, such as, II Timothy 1:7, "God hath not given us the spirit of fear; but of power, and of love and of a sound mind," Hebrews 11:6, "But without faith it is impossible to please God," and I John 5:18, "There is no fear in love; but perfect love casteth out fear: because fear hath torment. He that feareth is not made perfect in love."

Asking Amiss

In James 4:2-3 we see that we have not because we ask not and when we ask we ask amiss, "…Yet ye have not, because ye ask not. Ye ask, and receive not, because ye ask amiss, that ye may consume it upon your lusts." Asking amiss consists of praying a prayer that does not line up with the will of God. Often Believers become frustrated because their prayer has not been answered. The Believer should first be certain that their request is the will of God. If you know it is the will of God continue to wait on the Lord. Paul exhorts us in Galatians 6:9 to continue in faith when we believe God for something, "And let us not be weary in well doing: for in due season we shall reap, if we faint not."

Wavering

Again in James 1:21 we see that a person that wavers in their belief can not obtain the answer they seek. "…But let him ask in faith, nothing wavering. For he that wavereth is like a wave of the sea driven with the wind and tossed. For let not that man think that he shall receive anything of the Lord. A double minded man is unstable in all of his ways." If we are not sure of what we believe God for, or if we change our request daily, we will not receive the prayer request. Note the following example of wavering: Today I prayed and asked the Lord for a new home, at a certain address, for a certain amount and then tomorrow I pray, "If it is not your will God for me to have this kind of home I can stay where I am." In God's guidelines for receiving answers to prayers (the Bible) God says that a double minded person should not expect to receive anything from Him (James 1:26). You can not waver and expect to receive answers from God. Once the prayer has been prayed begin to thank God daily for the manifestation. Remember the example of Abraham in Romans 5:20, "He staggered not at the promise of God through unbelief, but was strong in faith, giving glory to God."

WRONG SEASON OR TIMING

We discussed earlier the importance of the right season. For example we know that Jesus was sent in the earth to fulfill the plan of God by going to the cross. In Luke 2:46 Jesus was found at the age of 12, "sitting in the midst of the doctors, both hearing them, and asking them questions." Jesus was only 12 years old but He was still called to be the Messiah although it wasn't the fullness of time. As a matter of fact He was called before the foundations of the world, even at birth He was the Messiah but He didn't walk into His true role or ministry until He was about 30 years old. The full scope of His ministry only lasted approximately 3 ½ years according to the scripture. But He could not begin his ministry until the right time or right season. We note Jesus walking into his season in Luke 4:18 when He stood and read from Isaiah 61:1-3; "The spirit of the Lord is upon me, because he hath anointed me to preach the gospel to the poor, he hath sent me to heal the brokenhearted, to preach deliverance to the captives and recovering of sight to the blind, to set at liberty them that are bound, to preach the acceptable year of the Lord… And he began to say unto them, This day is this scripture fulfilled in your eyes." Jesus read these scriptures as an indication that the Spirit of the Lord was upon Him, that it was His season for ministry. We are not to get discouraged in prayer if we don't receive an answer right away it could be that the season is not right. For example, a person could be praying for God to bless them with a million dollars. Although God is not opposed to His children becoming millionaires, the present season may be a season of preparation, a time to learn how to manage your bank account or balance your check book or a season to be found faithful over a little. You see God wants us to be mature and able to handle and keep the blessing before He pours out on us His promises. Imagine if God allowed this prayer to be answered and you were not properly prepared… It would be a disaster. Once again I must emphasis that knowing the right season is very important. There will be many times in prayer that you may sense God leading you in a certain way or direction and began to pray for that particular thing but, you must remember that our timing and God's timing is different. Therefore, never give up in prayer until you get the full manifestation of the prayer you prayed according to the Word of God. The Bible say's "let us not be weary in well doing: for in due season we shall reap if we faint not." (Galatians 6:9).

SCRIPTURE REFERENCE:

Hebrew 3:12

Habakkuk 2:4

Mark 6:6, 21-23, 16: 14

Matthew 13: 58, 17:20, 18: 21-22

James 4:2-3

I Corinthians 13

Galatians 6: 9-10

Hebrews 3:12, 19, 4: 6, 11

James 1: 21

Psalm 15: 1-5, 66: 18

Roman 1: 17, 5: 20, 14: 23

John 3: 16

Luke 2: 46, 4: 18

Isaiah 61: 1-3

I John 3: 22

Galatians 5:6

CHAPTER QUESTIONS

1. Name at least three hindrances to answered prayer:

    _____

    _____

2. Name the sin that is insidious and is most hated by God.

    _____

    _____

3. What sin greatly affects our ability to operate in faith?

    _____

    _____

4. Complete this scripture: "The Lord could do no mighty works because of their.."

    _____

    _____

5. What is one of the key things that bring power in prayer?

    _____

    _____

"The earnest (heartfelt, continued) prayer of a righteous man makes tremendous power available (dynamic in its working)"

JAMES 5:16
AMPLIFIED VERSION

CHAPTER 5

Different Types Of Prayer

A skillful person of prayer understands that the most strategic type of prayer is the right prayer for the specific need. There is not one type of prayer that covers every need. Therefore we must trust the Holy Spirit to give us the wisdom to pray the most effective prayer or prayers for our needs and the needs of others. Frequently all types of prayer have been misnamed as "Intercession," or it has been thought that intercession is the only effective kind of praying. But in reality, the most effective prayer is the prayer inspired by the Holy Spirit, whether it is the prayer of Agreement, the prayer of Faith, the prayer of Praise and Worship, or some other type of prayer. Often, different kinds of prayer will work together much like the fingers on a hand (1992 Kenneth E. Hagin, "The Art of Prayer"). The more you pray you will learn to flow in prayer using the right type of prayer without much thought by trusting the leading of the Holy Spirit. However as you are developing in prayer ask the Holy Spirit about the type of prayer that will be most effective. Below are examples of different types of prayers.

THE PRAYER OF FAITH

The prayer of faith is a prayer of petition, it is the prayer to change things. This prayer is always based on God's revealed will in His Word and never contains "if it be thy will" (1992 Hagin). Matthew 21:22 says "Verily I say unto you, If ye have faith, and doubt not, ye shall not only do this which is done to the fig tree, but also if ye shall say unto this mountain, Be thou removed, and be thou cast into the sea; it shall be done. And all things, whatsoever shall ask in prayer, believing ye shall receive." Again in Mark 11:24, Jesus said, "Therefore I say unto you, that what things soever ye desire, when ye pray, believe that ye receive them, and ye shall have them." The prayer of faith requires that we believe by faith and that what we pray is according to God's Word. Then we will obtain the answer to our prayer. I John 5: 14-15 the scriptures says, "And this is the confidence that we have in him, that if we ask any thing according to his will, he heareth us: And if we know that he hear us, whatsoever we ask, we know that we have the petitions that we desired of him. James referred to the prayer of faith in reference to praying for the sick in James 5: 16, "And the prayer of faith shall save the sick, and the Lord shall raise him up; and if he have committed sins, they shall be forgiven him."

One of the best examples I can recall in my own life is several years ago I had been in an automobile accident. A pick-up truck hit me head on as I stopped at a stop sign. Although I didn't get seriously hurt it had a tremendous emotional affect on me (I had previously been in several near death accidents in my life). After the accident I had difficulty sleeping. It did not matter how tired I was, as soon as the lights went out and I lay down, my eyes would pop wide open. This was very frustrating and irritating to me and my husband. I was seeing a doctor for the injury and he prescribed sleeping pills for me. He said I was suffering from a mild case of post traumatic stress syndrome. I took the pill one night and I did go to sleep. But down on the inside I knew if I started taking those pills I would have to take them every night. The next night I did not take the pills and once again I was wide awake. As I began to pray the Lord revealed that I was dealing with a spirit of fear. Later in that week I attended a business meeting at our church that Dr. Holt was holding. After the meeting was over I was about to leave and the Lord reminded me of my sleeping problem so, I went over to Dr. Holt and asked if she would lay hands on me and pray. She prayed the prayer of faith and that tormenting spirit left me immediately and I have not been tormented since. I sleep like a baby every night. Praise God!

THE PRAYER OF CONSECRATION

The prayer of consecration – Is a prayer of consecration and dedication of our lives for God's use. Jesus only used the phrase "if it be Thy will" when He prayed a prayer of consecration and dedication. In Luke 22:42 in the Garden of Gethsemane Jesus said, "Father, if thou be willing, remove this cup from me: nevertheless not my will, but thine, be done." In this scripture Jesus was not praying a prayer to change something. He was praying a prayer of consecration and dedication. When we use the phrase, "If it be thy will" in our prayers it is because we want to be available to do what Jesus wants us to do. We should be willing to go anywhere and do anything God has called us to do, whether it is to be a Pastor, a Prophet, a missionary, or a business owner or whatever God has called you to be. Therefore, in a prayer of dedication and consecration, we are to pray, "Lord, if it be Thy will" or "Lord, Thy will be done." However, when it comes to receiving something from God according to His Word, we do not pray, "If it be Thy will." We already know God's will because we have God's Word for it (1992 Hagin). It is God's will that our needs be met. God wants to give us what we need and we receive our needs met by faith.

THE PRAYER OF COMMITMENT

In the prayer of commitment we cast our cares upon the Lord. Paul gives us an example of this kind of prayer in Philippians 4:6 when he said, "Be careful for nothing; but in every thing by prayer and supplication with thanksgiving let your request be made known unto God." Then in 1 Peter 5:7 (Amplified version) Peter says, "Casting the whole of your care – all your anxieties, all your worries, all your concerns, once and for all – on Him; for He cares for you affectionately, and cares about you watchfully." As we cast our cares upon the Lord, we definitely commit our problems to Him. This is what it means to pray the prayer of commitment (1992 Hagin). Another example in scripture of casting our cares on the Lord is seen in the Old Testament in Psalm 37:5, "Commit thy way unto the Lord; trust also in him; and He shall bring it to pass." The margin of the King James translation says "Roll thy way upon the Lord." The words "cast," "commit," and "roll" are all words that convey the same thought. We are to simply cast or roll our cares upon the Lord (1992 Hagin).

THE PRAYER OF PRAISE AND WORSHIP

The prayer of praise and worship is a prayer where we minister to the Lord. In Acts 13: 1- 4, "Now there were in the church that was at Antioch certain prophets and teachers; as Barnabas, and Simeon that was called Niger, and Lucius of Cyrene, and Manaen, which had been brought up with Herod the tetrarch, and Saul. As they ministered to the Lord, and fasted, the Holy Ghost said, Separate me Barnabas and Saul for the work whereunto I have called them. And when they had fasted and prayed, and laid their hands on them, they sent them away. So they, being sent forth by the Holy Ghost, departed unto Selecia; and from thence they sailed to Cyprus. In this scripture we see the people were not petitioning God to do anything. But rather here it says they ministered to the Lord and fasted. Ministering to the Lord is the prayer of praise and worship. In Acts 13, we see the early church ministering to the Lord with the prayer of worship. And notice there is more than just a one-way conversation involved in this account in Acts 13, for it says, "As they ministered to the Lord, and fasted, the Holy Ghost SAID…" This is the prayer of worship (1992 Hagin). We note another example of the prayer of Praise and Worship in Acts 16:25, "And at midnight Paul and Silas prayed, and sang praises unto God." In both of these references we note that they were not singing or ministering one to another but unto God. The prayer of praise and worship is not asking God for anything but rather is a time of ministering to the Lord.

The Prayer of Agreement

The prayer of agreement is a powerful prayer and is often referred to as the "Keys to the Kingdom." In Matthew 18: 18-20, Jesus talking to the disciples and all the believers to come, said:

> *"Verily I say unto you, whatsoever ye shall bind on earth shall be bound in heaven; and whatsoever ye shall loose on earth shall be loosed in heaven. Again I say unto you, that if two of you shall agree on earth as touching anything that they shall ask, it shall be done for them of my Father which is in heaven."*

We also know that the scripture indicates that one can chase a thousand and two put ten thousand to flight in Deuteronomy 32:30. In other words, you can do ten times as much with someone agreeing with you as you can by yourself. There doesn't have to be a great number of people for the prayer of agreement to work. The prayer of agreement requires just two on earth, agreeing according to God's Word. The prayer of agreement can also be used when standing on a promise according to God's Word. You and God's Word are two in the earth.

PRAYER IN THE SPIRIT OR PRAYING IN UNKNOWN TONGUES
(I Corinthians 14:14, 15)

Prayer in other tongues, or often referred to as praying in the Spirit, is very important in obtaining answers in prayer and praying the perfect will of God (1992 Hagin). According to scripture in I Corinthians 14:2 "He that speaketh in an unknown tongue speaketh not unto men, but unto God; for no man understandeth him; howbeit in the spirit he speaketh mysteries." Also in Acts 2:4 we see believers receiving the Holy Ghost with the evidence of speaking in other tongues, "And they were all filled with the Holy Ghost, and began to speak with other tongues, as the Spirit gave them utterance." The Holy Spirit helps with our infirmities according to Romans 8:26-27:

> *"Likewise the Spirit also helpeth our infirmities: for we know not what we should pray for as we ought; but the Spirit himself maketh intercession for us with groanings which cannot be uttered. And he that searcheth the hearts knoweth what is the mind of the Spirit, because He maketh intercession for the saints according to the will of God."*

After we have prayed all that we know in an area of prayer, according to the scripture, we then pray in the spirit because the Holy Spirit helps us with our infirmities or weaknesses or those areas where we don't know what to pray. Praying in the Spirit or praying in tongues also is used in scripture to build the believer's spirit up in Jude 20, "But ye, beloved, building up yourselves on your most holy faith, praying in the Holy Ghost." Praying in tongues remains a controversial topic among Christians. However this topic is thoroughly discussed and substantiated in scripture and is truly the power source of a believer's life. Praying in tongues allows the believer to pray a prayer that is never understood by the devil and therefore can not be hindered. When a Christian prays in an unknown tongue it is a perfect language, perfect communication between the believer and the Father. All Believers should spend time daily praying in tongues. Remember Corinthian 14:2, "For he that speaketh in an unknown tongue speaketh not unto men, but unto God." What a privilege to be able to approach the holy throne of God and have an audience with the God of the universe. Remember Paul said that he prayed in tongues more than all of us and he wrote over two thirds of the bible. Hallelujah!! I believe the amount of time that Paul spent praying in the spirit, and in fellowship with God is one of the reasons he had such revelation. Praying in the spirit is for every believer, it is a gift from God.

UNITED OR CORPORATE PRAYER

The best example of united or corporate prayer in scripture is found in Acts 4:23-31, "And being let go, they went to their own company, and reported all that the chief priests and elders had said unto them. And when they heard that, THEY LIFTED THEIR VOICE WITH ONE ACCORD, and said, Lord, thou art God, which hast made heaven, and earth, and the sea, and all that in them is: Who by the mouth of thy servant David hast said, Why did the heathen rage, and the people imagine vain things? The kings of the earth stood up, and the rulers were gathered together against the Lord, and against his Christ. For of a truth against thy holy child Jesus, whom thou hast anointed, both Herod, and Pontius Pilate, with the Gentiles, and the people of Israel, were gathered together, for to do whatsoever thy hand and thy counsel determined before to be done. And now, Lord, behold their threatenings: and grant unto thy servants, that with all boldness they may speak thy word, by stretching forth thine hand to heal: and that signs and wonders may be done by the name of thy holy child Jesus. And WHEN THEY HAD PRAYED, THE PLACE WAS SHAKEN where they were assembled together; and they were all filled with the Holy Ghost, and they spake the word of God with boldness (1992 Hagin).

The Prayer of Supplication

The nature of supplication is much more heartfelt than a casual request. The word "supplication" means a humble, earnest entreaty or request. If a request is not made in a heartfelt, fervent, earnest manner, it would not be supplication. Repenting and confessing your sins is done by means of the prayer of supplication (1992 Hagin). We also pray the prayer of supplication to lift up the spiritual needs of others. Scriptural references to the prayer of supplication are found in Philippians 4:6, "Be careful for nothing; but by prayer and supplication with thanksgiving let your request be made known unto God." In Ephesians 6:18, "Praying always with all prayer and supplication in the Spirit, and watching thereunto with all perseverance and supplication for all saints." I Timothy 2:1-2, Paul exhort Timothy to pray, "First of all, supplications, prayers, intercessions, and giving of thanks, be made for all men; For kings, and for all that are in authority; that we may lead a quiet and peaceable life in all godliness and honesty."

Intercessory Prayer

Intercessory prayer is standing in the gap in prayer between a person or persons, who have provoked judgment upon themselves through their wrongdoing, and the actual execution of that judgment. Or to put it more simply, intercession is prayer to hold back judgment.

In 2003 a very close family member of mine had gotten heavily caught up in organized crime. At the time no one in my family nor I knew what he was up to. One night while relaxing and singing to the Lord, I closed my eyes to meditate on God's goodness. Suddenly, I had a vision of a person falling out of control into this huge inferno of fire. The place of fire was so large that as the person fell he looked like a small doll falling out of control off a two story building. I saw him hit the bottom and look around in terror at all the flames. Immediately I knew that it was the Lord leading me to pray for a soul that was falling quickly into hell. I began to cry out sincerely to God on behalf of that person's life. I pleaded to God that He would give him another opportunity to repent. As I prayed I recall asking the Lord to do whatever was necessary to prevent that person from going to hell. Then out of my spirit I prayed "arrest him in the spirit." In my mind that meant whatever it took, that person would be arrested in their sins. God assured me that the judgment of hell had been averted. At the time I did not really know who the person was but, after praying I had a strong sensing that it was my close family member. I picked up the phone and called that person and told them of the vision I had just had. Then by the leading of the Holy Spirit I warned them of impending judgment if they did not get out of whatever they were doing. They became very quiet and seemed surprised that the Lord had revealed to me they were involved in something ungodly. Six months later this person was arrested and was convicted of organized crime that involved several states. I remember crying to God to release him, to have mercy and not let him go to jail. Although he was wrong I pleaded for mercy. I did not want another family member to go to jail. As I cried before the Lord for his release the Lord reminded me of the vision almost six months before and said the alternative to jail for him would be hell. I was reminded that he could one day get out of jail but that hell was eternal. I praised God for His mercy.

To be effective, intercession needs to be made at the prompting of and under the direction of the Holy Spirit. (Genesis 18:16-33, Ezekiel 22:30, 31, Numbers 14:11-19, Exodus 32:7-14, Psalm 106:23).

SCRIPTURE REFERENCE

Matthew 18: 18-20, 21:22   Philippians 4:6
Acts 2:4, 4: 23-31   Genesis 18: 16-33
Mark 11:24   I Peter 5:7
Romans 8:26-27   Ezekiel 22: 30, 31
I John 5:14-15   Psalm 37:5
Jude 20   Numbers 14: 11-19
James 5:16   Acts 13:1-4, 16: 25
Ephesians 6:18   Exodus 32: 7-14
Luke 22:42   I Corinthians 14: 2, 14-15
I Timothy 2:1-2   Psalm 106: 23

CHAPTER QUESTIONS

1. Is there one type of prayer that works for every situation?

   _____

   _____

2. When is it scriptural to pray "If it be thy will Lord?"

   _____

   _____

3. Paul and Silas prayed at midnight in Acts 13: 1-4. What type of prayer did they pray?

   _____

   _____

4. According to scripture what is the evidence that a person is filled with the Holy Ghost.

   _____

   _____

5. Give a scriptural example of the prayer of supplication

   _____

Spend Quality time with Me and I will Pour more of My Life into you and Then you can Pour More Life into Others...

"...Out of his belly shall flow rivers of living water."
JOHN 7:38

CHAPTER
6

Spending Time With God

FELLOWSHIP

An effective person of prayer spends quality time on a daily basis with the Lord. The length of time is not as important as the quality and consistency of time. Spending time in the presence of the Lord helps the believer become more familiar with His voice and ways. John 10: 4-5 says, "And when he putteth forth his own sheep, he goeth before them, and the sheep follow him; for they know his voice, and a stranger will they not follow." The more time spent in the Word of God, in prayer, and in His presence, the easier it becomes to follow His leading. Often times we get so caught up in the routine of keeping a set schedule of prayer that it becomes a religious duty. Don't misunderstand me it is good to have a set time as you are establishing a life of prayer but, the next level is that you become so sensitive to God's leading that He can call on you to pray, to spend time with him whenever He needs you, whenever He calls you. When this occurs you will turn your favorite T.V. show off or push away your favorite meal to come away in His presence. When I first started praying I too had a difficult time keeping a scheduled prayer time. One day I heard someone talk about how it takes 21 days to break a habit. My heart immediately received that principle and I said to myself, if it takes 21 days to break a habit, I can also establish a habit in 21 days. So, guess what? I started setting the alarm clock for 5 am every morning for prayer. It was a very difficult task for me at first but, it became easier and easier and finally after 21 days, 5 am prayer had actually become a habit. This time worked very well for me at that time of my life. I soon began to notice the leading of the Lord to come away in prayer at different times of the day or night. My spirit had become more open, more sensitive to God. He could get my attention at anytime of the day (not just 5 am) and He was observing my obedience to pray. The anointing to intercede for others was developed and strengthen during these times. The Lord had established a relationship of trust with me in prayer. He could trust me to respond when he needed me. Remember God looks in the earth for people to intercede for men and women and children, to avert danger and destruction. Once the Lord has established that relationship of trust with you in prayer, you can be eating dinner and suddenly think about sister so and so and immediately you will recognize it is the Lord leading you to pray for her. Or you can be driving your car and pass another car and notice a person driving that reminds you of someone else and you will know it is the Lord leading you to pray for the person you thought you saw. The ultimate goal in prayer is to remain in constant communion, fellowship with the Lord. When this goal is established you will find yourself all through the day talking with the Lord in your spirit and Him talking back to you, about everything. When this occurs He doesn't have to get your attention to pray, your heart is always in a state of continual prayer and you dwell, live in His presence all the time.

Quality time in fellowship with the Father is extremely important in obtaining answers to prayer. If there is no relationship between you and the Holy Trinity, how can you be lead by the Spirit of God? The more time we spend getting to know the Lord and keeping His commandments, according to scripture, He will call us Friends. John 15: 14-15, "Ye are my friends, if ye do whatsoever I command you. Henceforth I call you not servants; for the servant knoweth not what his lord doeth: but I have called you friends; for all things that I have heard of my Father I have made known unto you." There are several references in scripture were God called His servants' friends. We note again in James 2:23 God referred to Abraham

84

as His friend, "Abraham believed God and it was imputed unto him for righteousness: and he was called the Friend of God."

Jesus left an example in the synoptic gospel of the kind of fellowship and relationship believers should have with God the Father. Jesus communed with God on a regular basis not because He had to, but because He wanted to be in the presence of His Father. "And in the morning, rising up a great while before day, He went out, and departed into a solitary place, and there prayed."(Mark 1:35). Jesus demonstrated for us in the gospels how we should live a successful Christian life. Often in scripture Jesus would pull aside, from His disciples and the crowd, to spend time with God. Mark 6:46, "And when he had sent them away, He departed into a mountain to pray." We note another example in Luke 5:16, "And He withdrew Himself into the wilderness and prayed." The Psalmist David said in Psalm 63:1, O God, thou art my God; early will I seek thee." David found the secret and joy of seeking the Lord early in the morning while everyone else was still sleeping. Throughout the scripture you see the sons of God seeking Him or spending quality time in His presence. Jesus proclaimed boldly in prayer to the Father in John 11: 41-42, "Father, I thank thee that thou hast heard me. And I knew that thou hearest me always." I think the reason Jesus was so confident that His Father heard Him was because of His daily relationship and time of communion with the Father. Jesus now desires to have a continuous relationship with each us according to Revelation 3:20, "Behold, I stand at the door, and knock; if any man hear my voice, and open the door, I will come in to him, and will sup with him, and he with me." The scripture also refers to true worshipers, those that seek the Lord and obey him, whom the Father seeks to worship Him, "But the hour cometh, and now is, when the true worshipers shall worship the Father in spirit and in truth: for the Father seeketh such to worship him." The Father actually is looking for those of us who chose to worship Him in spirit and truth. In Luke 1: 9-13 Zacharias and his wife Elisabeth had been seeking the Lord for a child. As Zacharias was seeking the Lord in Spirit and in Truth during his priestly duty, notice what happen: "But the angel said unto him, fear not, Zacharias: for thy prayer is heard; and thy wife Elisabeth shall bear the a son." The Lord answered the prayer of Zacharias, a worshiper. In the next chapter we will discuss guidelines for developing a daily relationship with the Lord through prayer and study of the word.

Listening to God

Often in prayer there is a lot of focus on what we say to God but, it is equally important to hear what God has to say to us. Listening is frequently an overlooked aspect of prayer. Remember prayer is communication between God and mankind. You may ask, "Does God really speak to man?" Yes God does speak to man by His word. Therefore, again there is great emphasis in knowing God's Word. If you don't know God's Word you won't recognize when He is talking to you. Nonetheless God has a way of communicating with his children. God can use anything He wants to get our attention. In Numbers 22: 28 God used a donkey to get the attention of His prophet. In Acts 9: 11-12 God sent Ananias to speak to Paul and give him direction. God is always talking, but the question is: Are we listening? Isaiah 30: 21 says "And thine ears shall hear a word behind thee, saying, This is the way, walk ye in it, when ye turn to the right hand, and when ye turn to the left." Spending quiet time listening, waiting on the Lord will bring growth and strength to the person of prayer. Finally, Isaiah 40:31 says, "But they that wait upon the Lord shall renew their strength; they shall mount up with wings as eagles; they shall run, and not be weary; and they shall walk, and not faint."

Fasting

Fasting can be a valuable tool used to quiet the flesh or carnal nature of man, which then allows us to hear clearly God's response to our prayer or instructions from Him. Although the believer has obtained salvation of the spirit man, the Holy Spirit is still at work on our soul. Remember the scripture refers to working out your own soul salvation. Although our spirits are saved, there is a daily renewing of the soul by the word of God. Fasting helps us to get our focus off "pleasurable" things we enjoy or desire and focus on "spiritual" areas of our life that are being refined. Fasting coupled with prayer generally will increase the response time to answered prayer. This increase in response is not because fasting moves God but, rather because our ability to hear and obey God is heighten when we fast. Fasting maximizes the influence of the spirit man. Fasting, by definition involves self denial, therefore fasting should be a purposeful denial of something you enjoy for a specified period of time. Generally when speaking of prayer most people think of giving up food, however there are a number of things a person could fast i.e., T.V., shopping, talking on the telephone. You can choose one day a week that you purpose to fast. The best person to consult regarding what you should fast is the Holy Spirit. Once you determine the specifics of your fast, lay it on the altar as a sacrifice before the Lord. In doing this you are saying to your soul that you are choosing to be led by the spirit not the flesh. Fasting will help bring the appetites of your flesh under control. In order to maintain consistency in your personal consecration to the Lord, I believe the fasted lifestyle works best. This means that you fast "something" each week. Always seek the Lord about what you should fast and be obedient to do it.

SCRIPTURAL REFERENCE
John 10: 4-5, 11: 41-42, 15: 14-15
James 2: 23
Mark 1: 35
Luke 5: 16
Psalm 63: 1
Revelation 3:20
Luke 1: 9-13
Numbers 22:28
Acts 9: 11-12
Isaiah 30:21, 40:31

CHAPTER QUESTIONS

1. List one thing that will increase your ability to hear the voice of God.

   _____

   _____

2. Name at least two people in scripture that God referred to as friends?

   _____

   _____

3. In John 15: 14-15 Jesus says that we would be His friend if we do what?

   _____

   _____

4. Prayer is two way communication between God and man. Which side of prayer often goes unattended?

   _____

   _____

5. What is the real benefit of fasting?

   _____

   _____

"Wherefore take unto you the whole armor of God, that ye may be able to withstand in the evil day, and having done all to stand"

Ephesians 6:13

CHAPTER 7

Preparing For Victory In Prayer

The person that seeks to gain answers in prayer must be a student of the Word and know what the will of the Lord is concerning God's Word. God answers prayers that are prayed according to His word. Therefore to know when the answer comes or to understand if your request is the will of the Lord, you must have a strong Word base. Remember the Word of God is the language of prayer. If you don't know the language you can't effectively communicate with the Lord in prayer. There are five areas that are needed to be an effective person of prayer; they all fit together like the fingers on your hand.

1. READING
2. STUDYING
3. MEDIATING
4. MEMORIZING
5. CONFESSION

The following sections are designed to equip you to become victorious in prayer. Victory in prayer is obtained when we receive answers to our prayers. Below is a guide that will daily assist in strengthening your life of prayer.

READING

There are many scriptural references to reading of the Word of God. Paul exhorted Timothy in I Timothy 4:13 to "…Give attendance to reading, exhortation, to doctrine." In Deuteronomy 17:19-20 Moses gives us seven reasons to read the Word of God: "…And it shall be with him, and he shall read there in all the days of his life: that he may learn: (1) to fear the Lord his God, (2) to keep all the words of this law and these statutes, (3) to do them: (4) that his heart be not lifted up above his brethren, (5) that he turn not aside from the commandments, to the right hand, or to the left; to the end (6) that he may prolong his days in his kingdom, and (7) that he and his children in the midst of Israel.

Remember the scriptures are to be read like reading a book. Of course during your reading time the Holy Spirit will illuminate certain words to you. You may ask, "How does the Holy Spirit illuminate words?" As you read the Word, there may be words that stand out although you may have read this same scripture before, but now it has a new meaning or it seems to come alive. As this occurs make a note to return after your reading assignment to further meditate and study that which was illuminated. As the Holy Spirit illuminates a word or scripture make a note in your journal and use these words or scriptures during your study time.

There are two Hebrew – Greek translations of the Word of God, "Logos" and "Rhema." The Logos word is the written scripture but the Rhema word is the spoken word of God according to Matthew 4: 4, "..Man shall not live by bread alone, but by every word that proceedeth out of the mouth of God." We read the logos daily, but when the Holy Spirit speaks to us through the written word, that spoken word is then a "rhema" word.

Make a commitment to God to read ten chapters a day. Remember according to Romans 8: 1 "there is therefore now no condemnation to them which are in Christ Jesus, who walk not after the flesh, but after the spirit." If you can't get through the ten chapters at first keep trying and increase by a chapter a day until you reach your goal. The reading assignment below is a monthly assignment that can be repeated each month. Repeating will also help you in the area of memorization. Also as you read the scriptures, out loud, and believe as you read, the scriptures will begin to get in your heart and become a part of your daily confession.

EXERCISE ASSIGNMENT
Ten Chapters A Day

Day 1 – Psalm 1-5, Ephesians 1-5
Day 2 – Psalm 6-10, Ephesians 6 – Phil. 1-4
Day 3 – Psalm 11-15, Colossians 1-4 –Thessalonians 1
Day 4 – Psalm 16-20, I Thessalonians 2-5 – II Thessalonians 1
Day 5 – Psalm 21-25, II Thessalonians 2-3 – I Timothy 1-3
Day 6 – Psalm 26-30, I Timothy 4-6, II Timothy 1-2
Day 7 – Psalm 31-35, II Timothy 3-4, Titus 1-3
Day 8 – Psalm 36-40, Philemon 1, Hebrews 1-4
Day 9 – Psalm 41-45, Hebrews 5-9
Day 10 – Psalm 46-50, Hebrew 10-13, James 1

Day 11 – Psalm 51-55, James 2-4, I Peter 1
Day 12 – Psalm 56-60, I Peter 2-5, II Peter 1
Day 13 – Psalm 61-65, II Peter 2-3, I John 1-3
Day 14 – Psalm 66-70, I John 4-5, II John, III John, Jude
Day 15 – Psalm 71-75, Acts 1-5
Day 16 – Psalm 76-80, Acts 6-10
Day 17 – Psalm 81-85, Acts 6-10
Day 18 – Psalm 86-90, Acts 16-20
Day 19 – Psalm 91-100, Acts 21-25

Day 20 – Psalm 101-105, Acts 26-28, Romans 1-3

Day 21 – Psalm 106-110, Romans 4-8
Day 22 – Psalm 111-115, Romans 9-13
Day 23 – Psalm 116-120, Romans 14-16, I Corinthians 1-2
Day 24 – Psalm 121- 125, I Corinthians 3-7
Day 25 – Psalm 126-130, I Corinthians 8-12
Day 26 – Psalm 131-135, I Corinthians 13-16, II Corinthians 1
Day 27 – Psalm 136-140, II Corinthians 2-6
Day 28 – Psalm 141-145, II Corinthians 7-11
Day 29 – Psalm 146-150, II Corinthians 12-13, Galatians 1-3
Day 30 – Proverbs 1-5, Galatians 4-6, Philippians 1-2
Day 31 – Proverbs 6-10, Philippians 3-4, Revelation 1-3

STUDYING

Paul exhorted Timothy to "Study to show thyself approved unto God a workman that needeth not to be ashamed, rightly dividing the word of truth." Studying is unlike reading the Word of God in that you take time to cross reference scripture, you allow the Holy Spirit to illuminate certain things to you. When a word or scripture is illuminated to you, go further in your study. For example going further may include using a concordance to find every where that word is used in the bible or cross-reference every where that same scripture is used. Also you may look up the Hebrew or Greek definition of a word to gain a better understanding of the use of the word in the text you may be studying. Additionally "Webster's" dictionary may be used to gain a better understanding of the meaning of a word. The word of God is full of life and you can gain new and fresh revelation every time you pick the Bible up. It is possible to spend hours, weeks, months, even years on the study of one topic. Remember as you spend time in the Word of God you are spending time with God and the more time spent with God in the

Word the stronger your relationship becomes with the Lord Jesus. The more time spent with the Lord you will begin to know His character and will be able to recognize what is of God and what is not of God. Subsequently, you become intimate with God and know what He likes and dislikes. Intimacy, knowing God, helps us to gain answers in prayer because we know His desires. Once we determine the desire of God in a situation we gain an advantage in prayer.

Basic Elements of Study

As you begin in the area of study it is important to realize that there are at least four basics elements of study according to Dr. Leo Holt: (2005 November, Bible Study, Dr. Leo Holt)

1. Repetition – Regularly channels the mind in a special direction so that habitual thought patterns can be formed.

2. Concentration – For study to be effective, it requires getting rid of distractions and focusing our attention completely on the Word of God for a given period of time.

3. Comprehension – There is something about repetition and focus that helps us comprehend the word as never before. Comprehension defines what you are studying.

4. Reflection – Reflection reveals the significance of what you're studying. In reflection we ponder the meaning of what we are studying until it causes us to see our world and ourselves in a new way.

When selecting an area of study ask the Holy Spirit which topics He would like you to begin studying. Remember the Holy Spirit is the Spirit of Truth and will lead you into all truth (John 16:13). It is best to be lead by the Spirit of God (Romans 8:14). I recommend you use this manual or purchase an additional notepad to make notes and write down scriptures for cross-reference. A good study bible will also aid in your study time. Keep your commitment to God daily and study to show yourself approved to God in the area of your study.

Below you will find some examples of topics for study:
1. Prayer
2. Fasting
3. Consecration
4. Love/Forgiveness
5. Miracles
6. Gifts of the Spirit
7. Ministry of Angels

MEDITATION

Meditation of the word of God is highly recommended. Find a scripture and read it over and over again. Close your eyes and think on that scripture. Ask the Holy Spirit to illuminate your mind, to enlighten the eyes of your understanding concerning that scripture. As you begin to practice meditating on the Word you will gain great revelation and insight into that scripture and you will also begin to prosper in that area. Why is it important to include meditation in our daily assignment? The answer is that Meditation brings revelation of the word of God. In Kenneth Hagin's "Bible Prayer Study Course," he talks about the impact that meditation can have on the believer. Below is an excerpt from his writings:

Meditation on the Word Brings Light

"Let me encourage you to meditate on the Word after you have studied it. Your spirit can be educated and trained. But just because you read the Word of God doesn't mean your spirit is educated. You can read the Bible and not understand what you're reading, and it won't mean a thing to you. The Word has to get down on the inside of you, in your heart or spirit. You get the revelation of the Word in your heart by meditating on it. When I was nineteen or twenty years old, I heard talk about Einstein's theory of relativity. I decided I would read it, since I'd heard so much about it. Before I read it, I didn't know a thing in the world about it. When I finished reading it, I knew less than I had before I read it! I think sometimes that's the way it is with people who read the Word of God. They know less when they finish reading it than they did when they began. They're trying to grasp the truth of God's Word with their minds. But you have to get the revelation of God's Word in your heart. After studying the Word, I would then shut my eyes and begin to meditate on the Word and just think about the scriptures I had been reading and studying. I've had a number of visions and revelations, but this revelation I had concerning the Name of Jesus was a revelation of the Word that any believer might have. The Holy Ghost will teach us the Word. As I meditated on the Word, on the inside of me I began to see something that I had never seen before."

(Copyright 1991 RHEMA Bible Church AKA Kenneth Hagin Ministries, Inc. Chapter 3, Praying in Jesus Name Part I, page 17)

There are numerous scriptures in the bible that encourage the believer to meditate on the word of God. In Joshua 1:8 the scriptures says

"This book of the law shall not depart out of thy mouth; but thou shall meditate therein day and night; that thou mayest observe to do according to all that is written therein: for then thou shalt make thy way prosperous, and then thou shalt have good success."

Daily during your time of study, meditate the word, and then take a scripture with you throughout the day and every moment you have meditate on it, read it over and over again. Meditate the Word of God.

EXAMPLES OF MEDITATION SCRIPTURE

Psalm 1:1-2 – *Blessed is the man that walketh not in the counsel of the ungodly, nor standeth in the way of sinners, nor sitteth in the seat of the scornful. 2) But his delight is in the law of the Lord; and in his law doth he meditate day and night.*

Isaiah 26:3 – *Thou wilt keep him in perfect peace, whose mind is stayed on thee: because he trusteth in thee.*

Philippians 4:8 – *Finally, brethren, whatsoever things are true, whatsoever things are honest, whatsoever things are just, whatsoever things are pure, whatsoever things are lovely, whatsoever things are of a good report; if there be any virtue, and if there be any praise, think on these things.*

I Timothy 4:15 – *Meditate upon these things; give thyself wholly to them; that thy profiting may appear to all.*

Psalm 119:15 – *I will meditate in thy precepts, and have respect unto thy ways.*

Psalm 119:97 – *O how I love thy law! It is my meditation all the day.*

Psalm 119:99 – *I have more understanding than all my teachers, for thy testimonies are my meditation.*

Psalm 63:6 – *When I remember thee upon my bed, and meditate on thee in the night watches.*

Psalm 77:12 - *I will meditate also of all thy work, and talk of thy doings.*

Psalm 143:5 – *I remember the days of old; I meditate on all thy works; I muse on the work of thy hands.*

Psalm 5:1 – *Give ear to my words, O Lord, consider my meditation.*

Psalm 19:14 – *Let the words of my mouth, and the meditation of my heart be acceptable in thy sight, O Lord, my strength, and my redeemer.*

Psalm 49:3 – *My mouth shall speak of wisdom: and the meditation of my heart shall be of understanding.*

Psalm 104:34 – *My meditation of him shall be sweet; I will be glad in the Lord.*

Psalm 119:23 – *Princes also did sit and speak against me; but thy servant did meditate in thy statutes.*

Psalm 119:48 – *My hands also will I lift up unto thy commandments, which I have loved; and I will meditate in thy statutes.*

Psalm 119:78 – *Let the proud be ashamed; for they dealt perversely with me without a cause: but I will meditate in thy precepts.*

Psalm 119:148 – *Mine eyes prevent the night watches, that I might meditate in thy word.*

There are many more scriptures on the topic of meditation. Here are a few for you to look up: Psalm 63:6, Psalm 119:23, 48, 78, and 148.

MEMORIZATION

Meditation and memorization go hand in hand. As a student of the Word, I recommend that as you prepare in school for testing, that you take the same sincerity in studying the Word of God. As you study and prepare in the Word you then become equipped for every test that God allows to come your way. Because the Word of God is our weapon, the sword of the spirit, we become highly dangerous to the enemy and his camp. Also we know from our study that God only hears and respond to His word in prayer, we become more effective in prayer. I recommend that you memorize scriptures on certain topics i.e., healing, prosperity, etc. Write down 3-5 scriptures a week on an index card and take them with you every where you go. Remember as you read these scriptures over and over that the Holy Spirit is truly the one to bring all things to your remembrance as you prepare yourself. As you study the word of God think of it like learning a new language all over again. You must study, read, meditate and memorize the scripture.

MEDITATION & MEMORIZATION ASSIGNMENT

Each week take at least one scripture a day from one topic and memorize and meditate for the entire day. Below you will find scriptural topics as well as a list of scriptures for each week to assist you in your development:

Week I – Strength
- Philippians 4:13 - *I can do all things through Christ who strengtheneth me.*

- Isaiah 30:15 - *For thus saith the Lord God, the Holy One of*

Israel; In returning and rest shall ye be saved; in quietness and in confidence shall be your strength.

- Ephesians 3:16,17 - *That he would grant you, according to the riches of his glory, to be strengthened with might by his spirit in the inner man, that Christ may dwell in your hearts by faith, that ye, being rooted and grounded in love.*

- Isaiah 40:31 - *But they that wait upon the Lord shall renew their strength; they shall mount up with wings as eagles, they shall run and not be weary; and they shall walk, and not faint.*

- Isaiah 41:10 - *Fear thou not; for I am with thee; be not dismayed; for I am thy God: I will strengthen thee; yea, I will help thee; yea, I will uphold thee with the right hand of my righteousness.*

- Isaiah 40:21 - *He giveth power to the faint and to them that have no might he increaseth strength.*

- Psalm 18:2 - *The Lord is my rock, and my fortress and my deliver; my God, my strength, in whom I will trust, my buckler, and the horn of my salvation, and my high tower.*

- Psalm 27:1 - *The Lord is my light and my salvation; whom shall I fear? The Lord is the strength of my life; of whom shall I be afraid?*

- Ephesians 6:10 - *Finally, my brethren, be strong in the Lord, and in the power of his might.*

Week II – Deliverance
- Exodus 3:8 – *And I am come down to deliver them out of the*

hand of the Egyptians, and to bring them up out of that land, unto a good land and a large, unto a land   flowing with milk and honey…

- Psalm 39:8 - *Deliver me from all my transgressions: make me not the reproach of the foolish.*

- Psalm 43:1 – *Judge me, O God, plead my cause against an ungodly nation: O deliver me from the deceitful and unjust man.*

- Psalm 56:13 – *For thou hast delivered my soul from death: wilt not thou deliver my feet from failing that I may walk before God in the light of the living.*

- Psalm 70:1 – *Make haste, O God, to deliver me; make haste to help me, O Lord.*

- Psalm 91:15 – *He shall call upon me, and I will answer him: I will be with him in trouble; I will deliver him and honor him.*

- Jeremiah 1:19 – *And they shall fight against thee; but they shall not prevail against thee; for I am with thee, saith the Lord, to deliver thee.*

- Psalm 32:7 – *Thou art my hiding place; thou shalt preserve me from trouble; thou shalt compass me about with songs of deliverance.*

Week III – Love
- Matthew 5: 44 - *But I say unto you, Love your enemies, bless them that curse you, do good to them that hate you, and pray for*

them which despitefully use you, and persecute you.

- Matthew 22: 37-40 - *...Thou shalt love the Lord thy God with all thy heart, and with all thy soul, and with all thy mind. This is the first and great commandment. And the second is like unto it, Thou shalt love thy neighbor as thyself. On these two commandments hang all the law and the prophets.*

- Romans 13:10 – *Love worketh no ill to his neighbour: therefore love is the fulfilling of the law.*

- Romans 12:9-10 – *Let love be without dissimulation. Abhor that which is evil: cleave to that which is good. Be kindly affectionate to one another with brotherly love; in love preferring one another.*

- Romans 5:5 – *And hope maketh not ashamed ; because the love of God is shed abroad in our hearts by the Holy Ghost which is given unto us.*

- Ephesians 3: 17 – *That Christ may dwell in your hearts by faith; that we being rooted and grounded in love, may be able to comprehend with all saints what is the breadth, and length, and depth, and height.*

- Ephesians 4:15 – *But speaking the truth in love, may grow up into him in all things, which is the head, even Christ.*

- Philippians 1:9-10 – *And this I pray that, your love may abound yet more and more in knowledge and in all judgement. That ye may approve things that are excellent; that ye may be sincere and without offense till the day of Christ.*

- I Peter 1:22 – *Seeing ye have purified your souls in obeying the truth through the Spirit unto unfeigned love of the brethren, see that ye love one another with a pure heart fervently.*

- I John 3:11 – *For this is the message that ye heard from the beginning, that we should love one another. Not as Cain, who was of that wicked one, and slew his brother. And wherefore slew he him? Because his own works were evil, and his brother's righteous. Marvel not, my brethren, if the world hate you. We know that we have passed from death unto life, because we love the brethren. He that loveth not his brother abideth in death.*

- I John 3: 23 – *And this is his commandment, That we should believe on the name of his Son Jesus Christ, and love one another, as he gave us commandment.*

- I John 4: 7 – *Beloved let us love one another; for love is of God; and every one that loveth is born of God, and knoweth God. He that loveth not knoweth not God; for God is love.*

- I John 4:20-21 – *If a man say, I love God, and hateth his brother, he is a liar: for he that loveth not his brother whom he hath seen, how can he love God whom he hath not seen? And this commandment have we from him, That he who loveth God love his brother also.*

Week IV – Mercy

- Numbers 14:18-19 – *The Lord is longsuffering, and of great mercy, forgiving iniquity and transgression, and by no means clearing the guilty, visiting the iniquity of the fathers upon the children unto the third and fourth generation. Pardon, I beseech thee, the iniquity of this people according unto the greatness of thy mercy, and as thou hast forgiven this people, from Egypt even until now.*

- Psalm 33:22 –*Let thy mercy, O Lord, be upon us, according as we hope in thee.*

- Psalm 61:7 – *He shall abide before God forever: O prepare mercy and truth, which may preserve him.*

- Psalm 62:12 – *Also unto thee, O Lord, belongeth mercy; for thou renderest to every man according to his work.*

- Psalm 103:11 – *For as the heaven is high above the earth, so great is his mercy toward them that fear him.*

- Micah 6:8 – *He hath showed thee, O man, what is good; and what doth the Lord require of thee, but to do justly, and to love mercy, and to walk humbly with thy God?*

- Matthew 5:7 – *Blessed are the merciful: for they shall obtain mercy.*

- Romans 9:23 – *And that he might make known the riches of his glory on the vessels of mercy, which he had afore prepared unto glory.*

- II Corinthians 4:1 – *Therefore having this ministry, as we have received mercy, we faint not.*

- Ephesians 2:4 – *But God, who is rich in mercy, for his great love wherewith he loved us.*

Week V – Healing

- Jeremiah 17:14 – *Heal me, O Lord, and I shall be healed: save me, and I shall be saved: for thou art my praise.*

- Jeremiah 30:17 – *For I will restore health unto thee, and I will heal thee of thy wounds...*

- Psalm 41:4 – *I said, Lord, be merciful unto me: heal my soul; for I have sinned against thee.*

- Hosea 6:1 – *Come, and let us return unto the Lord: for he hath torn, and he will heal us; he hath smitten and he will bind us up.*

- Hosea 14:4 – *I will heal their backsliding, I will love them freely; for mine anger is turned away from him.*

- Matthew 8:7 - *And Jesus saith unto him, I will come and heal him.*

- Matthew 10:1 – *And when he had called unto him his twelve disciples, he gave them power against unclean spirits, to cast them out, and to heal all manner of sickness and all manner of disease.*

- Luke 4:18 – *The Spirit of the Lord is upon me, because he hath anointed me to preach the gospel to the poor, he hath sent me to heal the brokenhearted, to preach deliverance to the captives, and recovering of sight to the blind, to set at liberty them that are bound.*

- Acts 4:30 – *By stretching forth thine hand to heal; and that signs and wonders may be done by the name of thy holy child Jesus.*

- Matthew 8:17 - *...Himself took our infirmities, and bare our sicknesses.*

- Matthew 8:16 – *When the even was come they brought unto him many that were possessed with devils; and he cast out the spirits with his word, and healed all that were sick.*

- Luke 4:40 – *Now when the sun was setting, all they that had any sick with divers diseases brought them unto him; and he laid his hands on every one of them, and healed them.*

- Luke 9:11 – *And the people, when they knew it, followed him: and he received them, and spake unto them of the kingdom of God, and healed them that had need of healing.*

- Acts 5:16 – *There came also a multitude out of the cities round about unto Jerusalem, bringing sick folks, and them which were vexed with unclean spirits and they were healed every one.*

- James 5:16 – *Confess your faults one to another, and pray one for another, that ye may be healed.*

- I Peter 2:24 – *Who his own self bare our sins in his own body on the tree that we, being dead to sins, should live unto righteousness: by whose stripes ye were healed.*

- Acts 10:38 – *How God anointed Jesus of Nazareth with the Holy Ghost and with power: who went about doing good, and healing all that were oppressed of the devil; for God was with Him.*

Week VI – Prosperity

- Psalm 118:25 – *Save now, I beseech thee, O Lord; O Lord, I beseech thee, send now prosperity.*

- Psalm 122:6,7 – *Peace be within thy walls, and prosperity within thy palaces.*

- Genesis 39:2-3 – *And the Lord was with Joseph, and he was a prosperous man... And his master saw that the Lord was with him, and that the Lord made all that he did to prosper in his hand.*

- Joshua 1:8 – *This book of the law shall not depart out of thy mouth; but thou shalt meditate therein day and night, that thou mayest observe to do according to all that is written therein: for then thou shalt make thy way prosperous, and then thou shalt have good success.*

- Isaiah 48:15 – *I, even I, have spoken; yea, I have called him; I have brought him, and he shall make his way prosperous.*

- Zechariah 8: 12 – *For the seed shall be prosperous; the vine shall give her fruit, and the ground shall give her increase, and the heavens shall give their dew; and I will cause the remnant of this people to possess all these things.*

- Genesis 24:40 – *And he said unto me, The Lord, before whom I walk, will send his angel with thee, and prosper thy way.*

- Genesis 39:23 – *And the keeper of the prison looked not to anything that was under his hand; because the Lord was with* him, and that which he did, the Lord made it to prosper.

- Deuteronomy 29: 9 – *Keep therefore the words of this covenant, and do them, that ye may prosper in all that ye do.*

- I King 2:3 – *And keep the charge of the Lord thy God, to walk in his ways, to keep his statues, and his commandments, and his judgements, and his testimonies, as it is written in the law of Moses, that thou mayest prosper in all that thou doest, and whithersoever thou turnest thyself.*

- II Chronicles 20:20 – *Believe in the Lord your God, so shall ye be established; believe his prophets, so shall ye prosper.*

- II Chronicles 26:5 – *And he sought God in the days of Zechariah, who had understanding in the visions of God; and as long as he sought the Lord, God made him to prosper.*

- Nehemiah 2:20 - *...The God of heaven, he will prosper us.*

- III John 2 – *Beloved, I wish above all things that thou mayest prosper and be in health, even as thy soul prospereth.*

- II Corinthians 9: 6-10 - *And God is able to make all grace abound toward you; that ye always having all sufficiency in all things, may abound to every good work.*

Week VII – Forgiveness
- II Corinthians 2: 10-11 – *To whom ye forgive any thing, I forgive also: for if I forgave anything, to whom I forgave it, for your sakes forgave I it in the person of Christ: Lest Satan should get an advantage of us; for we are not ignorant of his devices.*

- Colossians 3: 13 – *Forbearing one another, and forgiving one another, if any man have a quarrel against any; even as Christ forgave you, so also do ye.*

- Matthew 6: 12-15 – *And forgive us our debts, as we forgive our debtors… For if ye forgive men their trespasses, your heavenly Father will also forgive you; But if ye forgive not men their trespasses, neither will your Father forgive your trespasses.*

- Mark 11: 25-26 – *And when ye stand praying, forgive, if ye aught against any: that your Father also which is in heaven may forgive you your trespasses. But if ye do not forgive, neither will your Father which is in heaven forgive your trespasses.*

- Luke 6:37 – *Judge not, and ye shall not be judged: condemn not, and ye shall not be condemned: forgive and ye shall be forgiven.*

- Luke 11:4 – *And forgive us our sins; for we also forgive everyone that is indebted to us.*

- II Corinthians 2:7, 10 – *So that contrariwise ye ought rather to forgive him, and comfort him, lest perhaps such a one should be swallowed up with overmuch sorrow.*

- I John 1:9 – *If we confess our sins, he is faithful and just to forgive us our sins, and to cleanse us from all unrighteousness.*

- Ephesians 4: 32 – *And be ye kind one to another, tenderhearted, forgiving one another, even as God for Christ's sake hath forgiven you.*

- Colossians 2:13 – *And you, being dead in your sins and the uncircumcision of your flesh, hath he quicken together with him, having forgiven you all trespasses.*

- Colossians 1:14 – *In whom we have redemption through his blood, even the forgiveness of sins.*

Week VIII – Miracles

- John 2:11 – *This beginning of miracles did Jesus in Cana of Galilee, and manifested forth his glory and his disciples believed on him.*

- John 2:23 – *Now when he was in Jerusalem at the passover, in the feast day, many believed in his name, when they saw the miracles which he did.*

- John 6:2 – *And a great multitude followed him, because they saw his miracles which he did on them that were diseased.*

- Acts 2:22 – *Jesus of Nazareth, a man approved of God among you by miracles and wonders and signs, which God by him in the midst of you, as ye yourselves also know.*

- Acts 6:8 – *And Stephen, full of faith and power, did great wonders and miracles among the people.*

- Acts 8:6, 13 – *And the people with one accord gave heed unto those things which Phillip spake, hearing and seeing the miracles which he did.*

- Acts 15:12 – *Then all the multitudes kept silence, and gave audience to Barnabas and Paul, declaring what miracles and wonders God had wrought among the Gentiles by them.*

- Acts 19:11 – *And God wrought special miracles by the hands of Paul; so that from his body were brought unto the sick handkerchiefs or aprons, and the disease departed from them, and the evil spirits went out of them.*

- Hebrews 2:4 – *God also bearing them witness, both with signs and wonders and with divers miracles, and gifts of the Holy Ghost, according to his own will.*

- Mark 9:39 – *But Jesus said, Forbid him not: for there is no man which shall do a miracle in my name, that can lightly speak evil of me.*

- Acts 4:22 – *For the man was above forty years old, on whom this miracle of healing was showed.*

Week IX – Honor

- I Chronicles 29:12 – *Both riches and honor come of thee, and thou reignest over all; and in thine hand is power and might; and in thine hand it is to make great, and to give strength unto all.*

- II Chronicles 17:5 – *Therefore the Lord established the kingdom in his hand; and all Judah brought to Jehoshaphat presents; and he had riches and honor in abundance.*

- Psalm 8:5 – *For thou hast made him a little lower than the angels, and has crown him with glory and honor.*

- Psalm 91:15 – *He shall call upon me, and I will answer him: I will be with him in trouble; I will deliver him, and honor him.*

- Psalm 149:9 - *To execute upon them the judgement written: this honor have all his saints.*

- Proverbs 3:9 – *Honor the Lord with thy substance, and with the firstfruits of all thine increase.*

- Proverb 21:21 – *He that follows after righteousness and mercy findeth life, righteousness, and honor.*

- I Timothy 5:17 – *Let the elders that rule well be counted worthy of double honor especially they who labor in the word and doctrine.*

- II Timothy 2: 21 – *If a man therefore purge himself from these, he shall be a vessel unto honor, sanctified, and meet for the master's use, and prepared unto every good work.*

- I Peter 2:17 – *Honor all men, love the brotherhood. Fear God, Honor the king.*

Week X – Favor
- Esther 2:15 – *And Esther obtained favor in the sight of all them that looked upon her.*

- Esther 2: 17 – *And the King loved Esther above all the women, and she obtained grace and favor in his sight more than all the virgins.*

- Job 10:12 – *Thou has granted me life and favor, and thy visitation has preserved my spirit.*

- Psalm 5:12 – *For thou, Lord will bless the righteous; with favor wilt thou compass him as with a shield.*

- Psalm 30:5 – *For his anger endureth but a moment: and his favor is life: weeping may endure for a night, but joy cometh in the morning.*

- Psalm 102:13 – *Thou shalt arise and have mercy upon Zion: for the time to favor her, yea, the set time, is come.*

- Proverbs 8:35 – *For whoso findeth me, findeth life, and shall obtain favor of the Lord.*

- Proverbs 12:2 – *A good man obtaineth favor of the Lord: but a man of wicked devices will be condemned.*

- Proverbs 14:9 – *Fools make a mock at sin: but among the righteous there is favor.*

- Proverbs 14:35 – *The king's favor is toward a wise servant: but his wrath is against him that causeth shame.*

- Proverbs 16:15 – *In the light of the king's countenance is life: and his favor is as a cloud of the latter rain.*

- Proverbs 19:12 – *The king's wrath is as the roaring of a loin; but his favor is as dew upon the grass.*

- Proverbs 22:1 – *A good name is rather to be chosen than great riches, and loving favor rather than silver and gold.*

- Isaiah 60:10 – *And the sons of strangers shall build up thy walls, and their kings shall minister unto thee: for in my wrath I smote thee, but in my favor have I had mercy on thee.*

- Acts 7:46 – *Who found favor before God; and desired to find a tabernacle for God.*

CONFESSION

Confession is an important component of developing a strong prayer life. There are two methods of Confession that should be used daily. The first deals with our confession which must agree with whatever request we have asked of God. For example if we believe God for a healing we should not in our day to day conversation say things like "I am so sick of dealing with this," "If it is God's will I will just suffer." "I feel worst and worst each day." No, our conversation must line up with our confession or what we believe God for. For example our conversation actually should turn into our confession of faith. We should be saying things like, "I can do all things through Christ who strengthens me," "I am gaining strength each day," "I am already healed for the word says that by Jesus stripes I am already healed." The other method of Confession involves our purposeful confession of the word of God daily in words of faith and power. The second method will help you develop your daily conversation or confession. The more you confess the word the more it will get in your spirit and the more the word gets in your spirit the easier it will flow out of your mouth. Remember the scripture in Matthew that states "out of the abundance of the heart the mouth speaks." As you get the scripture in your mouth and in your heart about healing or what ever you believe God for, your manifestation will come forth quickly. Below you will find examples of daily confessions that will help edify and build your faith daily as you proclaim these confessions with boldness. As a daily exercise you may confess one subject each day of

115

the week or you may confess all subjects each day. As we daily confess the scripture for our spiritual edification remember to personalize the scripture. For example when you confess the word of God put your own personal name in the confession or "I" or "me." When believing God in certain areas search the scriptures for the words of God that apply to your life's situation. Remember the words of God are spirit and they are life (John 6: 63) and Jesus Christ (The anointed Word of God) is the same yesterday, and today, and forever (Hebrew 13:8). The word of God will never lose its power but it is up to us to believe and apply the Word to our day to day situations.

EXAMPLES OF CONFESSIONS

SPIRITUAL EDIFICATION

Ephesians 1: 3-21 - Blessed be the God and father of my Lord Jesus Christ, who hath blessed me with all spiritual blessings in heavenly places in Christ. According as he hath chosen me in him before the foundation of the world, that I should be holy and without blame before him in love. Having predestinated me unto the adoption of children by Jesus Christ to himself, according to the good pleasure of his will to the praise of the glory of his grace, wherein he hath made me accepted in the beloved. In whom I have redemption through his blood, the forgiveness of sins, according to the riches of his grace wherein he hath purposed in himself; That in the dispensation of the fullness of times he might gather together in one all things in Christ both which are in heaven and which are on earth; even in him In whom also I have obtained an inheritance, being predestinated according to the purpose of him who worketh all things after the counsel of his will: That I should be to the praise of his glory, who first trusted in Christ. In whom I also trusted, after that ye heard the word of truth the gospel of your salvation: in whom also after that I believed I was sealed with the Holy Spirit of promise which is the earnest of my inheritance until the earnest of my inheritance until the redemption of the purchased possession, unto the praise of his glory. I pray that the God of my Lord Jesus Christ, the Father of glory, may give unto me the spirit of wisdom and revelation in the knowledge of him: The eyes of my understanding being enlightened that ye may know what is the hope of his calling, and what the riches of the glory of his inheritance in the saints And what is the exceeding greatness of his power to us-ward who believe, according to the working of his mighty power which he wrought in Christ, when he raised him from the dead, and set him at his own right hand, in the heavenly places Far above all principality and, power, and might and dominion and every name that is named, not only in this world, but also in that which is to come.

Ephesians 3:14-20 - *"For this cause I bow my knees unto the Father of our Lord Jesus Christ, 15) of whom the whole family in heaven and earth is named, 16) That He would grant unto me according to the riches of his glory, to be strengthened with might by his Spirit in my inner man; 17) That Christ may dwell in my heart by faith; that I being rooted and grounded in love, 18) May be able to comprehend with all saints what is the breadth, and length, and depth, and height; 19) And to know the love of Christ, which passeth knowledge, that I might be filled with all the fullness of God. 20) Now unto him that is that worketh in me."*

Ephesians 4:22-32 - *"I pray that I put off concerning the former conversation the old man which is corrupt according to the deceitful lusts; 23) And I will be renewed in the spirit of my mind: 24) And that I put on the new man, which after God is created in righteousness and true holiness. 25) Wherefore I will put away lying, I will speak the truth with my neighbor: For we are members one of another: 26) And I shall not be angry, and I shall sin not, neither shall I let the sun go down upon my wrath: 27) Neither shall I give place to devil 28) I shall not steal but rather labor working with my hands the thing which is good, that I may have to give to him that needeth. 29) I will let no corrupt communication proceed out of my mouth, but that which is good to the use of edifying, that it may minister grace unto* the hearers. 30) And I will not grieve not the Holy Spirit of God, whereby I am sealed unto the day of redemption. 31) I will let all bitterness and wrath, and anger, and clamor, and evil speaking be put away from me with all malice 32) And I shall be kind, tenderhearted, forgiving one another, even as God for Christ's sake hath forgiven me."

Philippians 1:10-11 - *"I pray that I may approve things that are excellent that I may be sincere and without offense till the day of Christ; being filled with the fruits of righteousness, which are by Jesus Christ, unto the glory and praise of God."*

Philippians 2:13-15 - *"For it is God which worketh in me both to will and to do his good pleasure. I will do all things without murmurings and disputings: That I may be blameless, the son of God without rebuke, in the midst of a crooked and perverse nation, among whom I shall shine as a light in the world."*

Philippians 4:4-8 - *"I will rejoice in the Lord always and again I say I will rejoice. I will let my moderation be known unto all men. I will be careful for nothing; but in every thing by prayer and supplication with thanksgiving I will make my request known unto God. And the peace of God, which passeth all understanding shall keep my heart and mind through Christ Jesus. Finally whatsoever things are true, whatsoever things are honest, whatsoever are just, whatsoever things are pure, whatsoever things are lovely, whatsoever things are of a good report, if there be any virtue, and if there be any praise think on these things."*

Colossians 1:9-14 - *"For this cause I also, since the day I heard it, I do not cease to pray and to desire that I might be filled with the knowledge of his will in all wisdom and spiritual understanding. That I might walk worthy of the Lord unto all pleasing, being fruitful in every good work, and increasing in the knowledge of God; being also strengthened with all might, according* to his glorious power, unto all patience and longsuffering with joyfulness; giving thanks unto the Father, which hath made me meet to be a partaker of the inheritance of the saints in light: Who hath delivered me from the power of darkness, and hath translated me into the kingdom of his dear Son; In whom I have redemption through his blood, even the forgiveness of sins."

Colossians 2:12-15 - *"Because I was buried with Him in baptism, wherein also I was risen with Him through the faith of the operation of God, who hath raised him from the dead. And I being dead in my sins and the uncircumcision of my flesh, hath he quickened together with Him, having forgiven me my trespasses; blotting out the hand writing of ordinances that was against me which was contrary to me, and took it out of the way, nailing it to the cross; and having spoiled principalities and powers, Jesus made a show of them openly, triumphing over them in it."*

Colossians 3:12-17 - *"I will put on therefore, as the elect of God, holy and beloved bowels of mercies kindness, humbleness of mind, meekness, longsuffering; Forbearing one another, and forgiving one another, if any man have a quarrel against any: even as Christ forgave me, so also will I. And above all these things I will put on charity, which is the bond of perfectness. And let the peace of God rule your heart to the which also I am called in one body and I shall be thankful. I will let the word of Christ dwell in me richly in all wisdom, teaching and admonishing one another in psalms and hymns and spiritual songs, singing with grace in my heart to the Lord. And whatsoever I do in word or deed, do all in the name of the Lord Jesus, giving thanks to God and the Father by Him."*

Isaiah 11:2-3 - *"And the spirit of the Lord shall rest upon me, the spirit of wisdom and understanding, the spirit of counsel and might, the spirit of knowledge and the fear of the Lord: And God shall make me of quick understanding in the fear of the Lord: and I shall not judge after the sight of my eyes, neither reprove after the hearing of the ears: But with righteousness shall judge the poor, and reprove with equity for the meek of the earth."*

PRAYERS OF PROTECTION

Ephesians 6:10 - *"I am strong in the Lord, and in the power of his might. Put on the whole armor of God, that I may be able to stand against the wiles of the devil 12) for I wrestle not against flesh and blood, but against principalities, against powers, against the rulers of the darkness of this world, against spiritual wickedness in high places. 13) wherefore I will take unto myself the whole armor of God, that I may to withstand in the evil day, and having done all, I will stand 14) I will stand therefore, having my loins girt about with truth, and having on the breast plate of righteousness 15) And my feet shod with preparation of the Gospel of peace; 16) Above all taking the shield of faith, wherewith I shall be able to quench all the fiery darts of the wicked. 17) And take the helmet of salvation and sword of the spirit which is the word of God; 18) praying always with all prayer and supplication in the spirit and watching thereunto with all perseverance and supplication for all saints."*

Psalm 91 - *"Because I dwell in the secret place of the most High, I shall abide under the shadow of the almighty. I will say of the Lord, He is my refuge and my fortress: my God; in him I will trust. Surely he shall deliver me from the snare of the fowler, and from the noisome pestilence. He shall cover me with his feathers, and under his wings shall I trust: his truth shall be my shield and buckler. I shall not be afraid for the terror by night; nor for the arrow that flieth by day; Nor for the pestilence that walketh in darkness; nor for the destruction that wasteth at noonday. A thousand shall fall at my side, and ten thousand at my right hand; but it shall not come nigh me. Only with my eyes shall I behold and see the reward of the wicked. Because I have made the Lord, which is my refuge, even the most High, my habitation. There shall no evil befall me, neither shall any plague come nigh thy dwelling. For he shall give his angels charge over me, to keep me in all my ways. They shall bear me up in their hands, lest I dash my foot against a* stone. I shall tread upon the lion and the dragon shall I trample under feet. Because I have set my love upon God, therefore he will deliver me and set me on high, because I hath known His name. I shall call upon God, and He will answer me. He will be with me in trouble; he will deliver me and honor me. With long life will he satisfy me and show me his salvation."

Psalm 27 - "The Lord is my light and my salvation; whom shall I fear? The Lord is the strength of my life; of whom shall I be afraid? When the wicked, even my enemies and my foes, came upon me to eat up my flesh, they stumbled and fell. Though a host should encamp against me, my heart shall not fear: though war should rise against me, in this I will be confident. One thing have I desired of the Lord, that will I seek after; that I may dwell in the house of the Lord all the days of my life, and to behold the beauty of the Lord , and to inquire in his temple. For in the time of trouble he shall hide me in his pavilion: in the secret of his tabernacle shall he hide me; he shall set me up upon a rock. And now shall mine head be lifted up above mine enemies round about me: therefore will I offer in his tabernacle sacrifices of joy; I will sing, yea, I will sing praises unto the Lord. Hear O Lord, when I cry with my voice: have mercy also upon me, and answer me. When thou saidst, Seek ye my face; my heart said unto thee, Thy face, Lord, will I seek. Hide not thou face far from me; put not thy servant away in anger: thou hast been help; leave me not, neither forsake me, O God of my salvation. When my father and my mother forsake me, then the lord will take me up. Teach me thy way, O Lord, and lead me in a plain path, because of mine enemies. Deliver me not over unto the will of mine enemies: for false witnesses are risen up against me, and such as breathe out cruelty. I had fainted, unless I had believed to see the goodness of the Lord in the land of the living. I will wait on the Lord. I will be of good courage, and God will strengthen my heart: I will wait on the Lord."

Isaiah 54:14-15, 17 - "In Righteousness I shall be established: I shall be far from oppression; for I shall not fear: and from terror; for it shall not come *near me. Behold they shall surely gather together, but not by me: whosoever shall gather together against me shall fall for my sake. No weapon that is formed against me shall prosper; and tongue that shall rise against me in judgement I shall condemn. This is the heritage of the servants of the Lord, and their righteousness is of me, saith the Lord."*

As mentioned earlier all five of these areas (reading, studying, meditation, memorization, and confession) are important and work together like the fingers on your hand. It is necessary to have a healthy balance of all five areas to be most effective not only in prayer but to live successfully as a Christian. Consistent use of these will strengthen the prayer life of the believer. Just as in our physical diet we must have a healthy balance of the different food groups, the same is true in order to have a healthy spiritual diet. If in our spiritual diet we read the word all the time and never study, we would be missing vital spiritual nutrients necessary to live a healthy spiritual life and eventually may develop some type of spiritual disease due to insufficient nutrients. Some of the possible spiritual diseases could be unbelief, pride, and fear; all of which could hinder our spiritual growth or even stunt our growth. As believers we should daily, read the word, study the word as well as meditate/memorize the word and then there must be a concentrated time of confession. Confession should also be a part of our daily conversation. Let me encourage you to not be overwhelmed. Take each day step by step and ask the Holy Spirit to guide and to help you. Also remember that these steps are only a suggested guide to developing a strong prayer life. If you are not able to follow the guidelines start were you are and remain consistent and faithful and the Lord will direct you.

"And this is the confidence
that we have in Him,
that if we ask anything
according to His will,
He hears us."

I John 5:14

CHAPTER 8

Conclusion

God is a faithful Father and He desires to answers our prayer and meet our every need. However, God does not answer all prayer but only those prayers that are scripturally based and are according to the perfect will of God for our lives. In addition, there are certain keys or guidelines in the Word of God that should be used as a guide. Also we looked at a few things that could possibly be responsible for hindered or unanswered prayer. The main key found from searching the scriptures is that if we know the will of God on a situation then we can know for sure He will answer our request. I John 5: 14-15 supports God answering our prayer, "And this is the confidence that we have in him, that, if we ask anything according to his will, he heareth us: And if we know that he hear us, whatsoever we ask, we know that we have the petitions that we desire of him." As Believers we trust our heavenly Father to answer our request and He will do just that. Many times we pray for things that are not according to His will. Christians must realize that God will only give the things that are "good" in light of eternity. He will give only what is eternally "good," and according to the execution of His plan and timetable for the whole world. "Good" for the believer may not be what he/she desires, but is that which God has established as the thing which will execute His plan and bring the believer into a closer relationship with Him. Additionally the guidelines in this Prayer Manual are designed to help the Believer become stronger and more balanced in the Word of God thereby becoming a more effective person of prayer.

Authors Bio

Doris Riley is called to preach and teach God's Word to the body of Christ. She is an Author and a Playwright. She has ministered healing to the lost and hurting for over 15 years. She is a Registered Nurse and has ministered life to thousands that were wounded physically, mentally and spiritually. God has blessed her to minister to his treasures of the earth; the lost, the homeless, the mentally ill and those in prison. Doris is a licensed Minister of the Gospel through Grace Christian Fellowship Church International and holds a Master of Biblical Counseling from Friends International Christian University, Merced, CA. Her life of prayer has been established through the things she has suffered personally, through praying for others, and a strong foundation in the Word of God. God has healed, delivered and set many free through her availability to Him to pray for others.

Doris is presently CEO and Cofounder with her husband Joseph Riley of: **Shekinah Prison Ministries,** a nonprofit organization designed to assist in meeting the needs of children and or families of those incarcerated. Throughout the year Shekinah Prison Ministries assist children/families who have suddenly found themselves in great need related to a parent or spouse incarcerated. Annually Shekinah Prison Ministries provide gifts during the holiday for children of those incarcerated all over the country.

Shekinah Productions, Inc. *(Encountering God in the Theater),* delivers a message to the lost and hurting through Christian productions including, prophetic dance, drama, plays and skits.

TESTIMONIES

*My husband and I were at our wits end, we had done everything to get pregnant to no avail. We had never taken fertility drugs and were at the stage where I needed to take my temperature frequently to determine when I was most fertile. Ms. Riley came in the office one day and I overheard her talk about what God was doing and that He still performed miracles. I heard her say that there was nothing to hard for God. I stood up from my desk and began to listen more intently. She laid her hands on me and prayed that God would open my womb. In less than six weeks I discovered I was pregnant and not only pregnant but, they discovered that I was pregnant with **triplets**. I thank God for my beautiful babies they are healthy and doing well. God made up for all the years we couldn't have children.*

P. Tripp, Memphis, TN

I called one day to speak with Ms. Riley about a job. During the conversation I mentioned that I had a large knot on my chest that had suddenly appeared. The knot was large and very painful. The doctor could not explain what it was. As I mentioned this, she asked if she could pray for me and I agreed. When she prayed I sensed the presence of God but nothing happened. The next morning I was sitting on my front porch enjoying the fresh air when all of a sudden I noticed that my blouse was wet and something was running down my chest. I rushed to the bathroom to check it out and discovered that the knot had burst and all the fluid had ran out. I was back to normal by the power of God. To God be all the glory.

E. Goolsby, Memphis, TN

For booking or donations, contact or e-mail:
shekinahprisonministries@yahoo.com – Fax # 662-504-4234
www.shekinahprisonministries.org